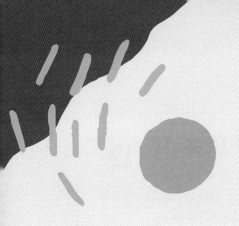

# Idea Garden

## –First Steps in Paragraph Writing–

Magda L. Kitano

## 音声再生アプリ「リスニング・トレーナー」を使った音声ダウンロード

朝日出版社開発のアプリ、「リスニング・トレーナー（リストレ）」を使えば、教科書の音声をスマホ、タブレットに簡単にダウンロードできます。どうぞご活用ください。

### ◉ アプリ【リスニング・トレーナー】の使い方

**《アプリのダウンロード》**

App Store または Google Play から「リスニング・トレーナー」のアプリ（無料）をダウンロード

App Storeは
こちら▶

Google Playは
こちら▶

**《アプリの使い方》**

① アプリを開き「コンテンツを追加」をタップ
② 画面上部に【15706】を入力しDoneをタップ

---

## 音声ストリーミング配信 》》》

この教科書の音声は、右記ウェブサイトにて無料で配信しています。

https://text.asahipress.com/free/english/

---

表紙デザイン：小林正明

# Preface

In your English classes until now, have you had a problem thinking of ideas for topics? For example, if the teacher tells you to talk freely in English with your partner, can you always find interesting things to talk about together? When you must write your opinion in English about an issue, have you ever had trouble writing because you don't have a strong opinion about that topic? If so, you're not alone. Communicating is something that we do when we have something to say, so it's unnatural to suddenly have to speak with a classmate only because we are sitting in an English class.

We need to practice using a foreign language in order to master it, but to practice it we also need something to say. *Idea Garden* is designed to help you with that. Each passage gives rich information about the unit's topic. Organizing this information gives us a clear framework to decide whether we agree or disagree with the writing topic. We can then use the organized information as support when we write a paragraph.

Following the instructions for each unit will guide you in this process, but two aspects of this textbook in particular will make your experience even more successful. First, throughout the book, students are encouraged to research the topics more on the internet. You can research in English or in Japanese, but finding out more about the topics can give you more to write about. Don't stop with just what you know or what is in the passage. Second, work together with your classmates. Writing is an individual activity, but brainstorming the topic before writing can result in many more ideas than what any one student could think up on their own. Do take advantage of the pair, group, and class-wide activities. Coming up with just enough ideas to write a paragraph will give you a good result, but starting with more than enough ideas will allow you to choose those that best fit how you feel about the topic.

The lessons of *Idea Garden* teach writing, and guide you in writing English paragraphs. But the process of organizing information from what you read and shaping that into structured output can be used both in school as well as in your future career.

Magda L. Kitano

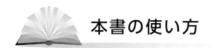

# 本書の使い方

◆**Conversation Box**

各ユニット最初のページでは、タイトル、写真、そして二つの質問により、各ユニットのテーマを紹介しています。質問について、クラスメートと自由に英語で会話をしましょう。

◆**Do you know these words?**

リーディングパッセージで使われている単語を、本文を読む前に確認しましょう。本文を読む際にも、この単語に注目しましょう。また、ライティングで必要なときに使うようにしましょう。

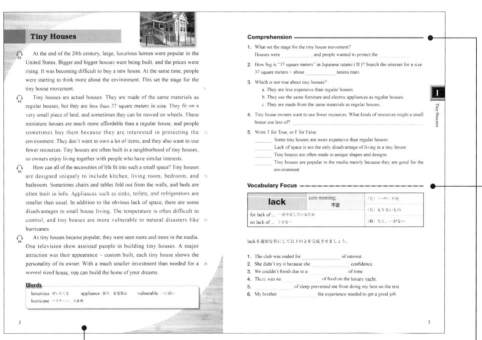

◆**Reading**

本文はライティングの素材になるので、内容をしっかり読みましょう。

◆**Comprehension**

異なる形式の質問で、本文の内容を確認したり、テーマについて考えたりします。必ずインターネットを使って調べる質問があるので、本文のテーマについて複数の方法で情報を集めましょう。

## ◆Vocabulary Focus

本文に出てきた単語を一つ、重点的に学習します。よく使われている単語こそ、意味や使い方の数が多いので、ここで知識を広げましょう。

## ◆Thinking about the Topic

このページでは、次のページのライティングの準備をします。本文の情報を整理したり、インターネットを使って更に情報を集めたりします。メモは完全文で書かなくてもいいのですが、英語で書いた方がライティングのときに書きやすくなります。ブレーンストーミングはグループで行うと、よりたくさんのアイディアを集めることができます。

## ◆Writing

ライティングの目標は、ユニット1〜4はセンテンス、ユニット5〜7は複数のセンテンス、ユニット8〜12はパラグラフ、ユニット13〜15は複数パラグラフライティングの一部です。Thinking about the Topicで準備をした情報を整理して完全文で書くことで、上手なライティングが出来上がります。

## ◆Reading Focus / Writing Focus

リーディング、ライティングに役立つテーマを紹介しています。ライティングの準備と執筆の際に、ここで紹介するポイントを使いましょう。

# CONTENTS

 **Unit 1** # Tiny Houses

**Conversation Box:**

❖ Where do you want to live in the future?

❖ Do you want to own your own house someday?

## Do you know these words?

すでに知っている単語の□にチェック印✓を書いて、下の意味と線で結びましょう。なお、分からない単語があれば辞書を使って、全ての単語を線で結びましょう。

☐ miniature     ☐ obvious     ☐ disaster     ☐ assist     ☐ investment

● help    ● easy to see    ● very small    ● an amount of money    ● a natural event that causes damage

# Tiny Houses

**02** At the end of the 20th century, large, luxurious homes were popular in the United States. Bigger and bigger houses were being built, and the prices were rising. It was becoming difficult to buy a new house. At the same time, people were starting to think more about the environment. This set the stage for the tiny house movement. 5

**03** Tiny houses are actual houses. They are made of the same materials as regular houses, but they are less than 37 square meters in size. They fit on a very small piece of land, and sometimes they can be moved on wheels. These miniature houses are much more affordable than a regular house, and people sometimes buy them because they are interested in protecting the 10 environment. They don't want to own a lot of items, and they also want to use fewer resources. Tiny houses are often built in a neighborhood of tiny houses, so owners enjoy living together with people who have similar interests.

**04** How can all of the necessities of life fit into such a small space? Tiny houses are designed uniquely to include kitchen, living room, bedroom, and 15 bathroom. Sometimes chairs and tables fold out from the walls, and beds are often built in lofts. Appliances such as sinks, toilets, and refrigerators are smaller than usual. In addition to the obvious lack of space, there are some disadvantages to small house living. The temperature is often difficult to control, and tiny houses are more vulnerable to natural disasters like 20 hurricanes.

**05** As tiny houses became popular, they were seen more and more in the media. One television show assisted people in building tiny houses. A major attraction was their appearance – custom built, each tiny house shows the personality of its owner. With a much smaller investment than needed for a 25 normal sized house, you can build the home of your dreams.

## Words

| | | |
|---|---|---|
| luxurious ぜいたくな | appliance 器具、家電製品 | vulnerable …に弱い |
| hurricane ハリケーン、大暴風 | | |

## Comprehension

1. What set the stage for the tiny house movement?

   Houses were _____, and people wanted to protect the _____.

2. How big is "37 square meters" in Japanese tatami (畳)? Search the internet for a size.

   37 square meters = about _____ tatami mats

3. Which is not true about tiny houses?

   a. They are less expensive than regular houses.

   b. They use the same furniture and electric appliances as regular houses.

   c. They are made from the same materials as regular houses.

4. Tiny house owners want to use fewer resources. What kinds of resources might a small house use less of? _____

5. Write T for True, or F for False.

   _____ Some tiny houses are more expensive than regular houses.

   _____ Lack of space is not the only disadvantage of living in a tiny house.

   _____ Tiny houses are often made in unique shapes and designs.

   _____ Tiny houses are popular in the media mainly because they are good for the environment.

## Vocabulary Focus

| **lack** | core meaning: 不足 | （名）（…の）不足 |
|---|---|---|
| | | （名）足りないもの |
| for lack of ... …が不足しているため <br> no lack of ... 十分な… | | （動）欠く、…がない |

lackを適切な形にして以下の文を完成させましょう。

1. The club was ended for _____ of interest.
2. She didn't try it because she _____ confidence.
3. We couldn't finish due to a _____ of time.
4. There was no _____ of food on the luxury yacht.
5. _____ of sleep prevented me from doing my best on the test.
6. My brother _____ the experience needed to get a good job.

## Thinking about the Topic

1. Tiny house に住む良い点と悪い点をパッセージから探して、表に書きましょう。

| Good points | Bad points |
|---|---|
| 例）low cost | |

2. パッセージに載っていないTiny house に住む良い点と悪い点を考えてみましょう。

| Good points | Bad points |
|---|---|
| | 例）maybe can't have a pet |

3. これらの良い点と悪い点を考えた上で、Tiny house に住みたいと思いますか？
   Would you like to live in a tiny house?　　　□　Yes.　　□　No.

4. グループになってアイディアを共有しましょう。
   - 自己紹介をする
   - Tiny house に住みたいかどうか
   - 上の表から一番そう思う理由を言う

   他のメンバーから良いアイディアを聞いたら
   1と2に書き加えましょう。

Try to speak
in all
English!

4

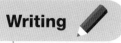
## Writing

Topic: Would you like to live in a tiny house?

**5.** このトピックについて自分の考えを選んでください:
- ☐ I would like to live in a tiny house.
- ☐ I wouldn't like to live in a tiny house.

**6.** 前のページの1と2から、上記の5で選んだ考えをサポートする理由を完全文で書いてみましょう。言いたいことを、パターン1,2,3を使って、それぞれ書きましょう。

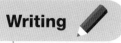

**PATTERN 1** 「Tiny houseは」　　　　　　　　　　　　　　　　【Yes/No】

| ex. low cost → | Tiny houses | cost | less than regular houses. | YES |
| ex. cute items → | Tiny houses | have | cute sinks, toilets, and refrigerators. | YES |
| | 複数形 | 現在形 | 複数形 | |

**Your sentence:**    Tiny houses _____

**PATTERN 2** 「～をしたいから」

| ex. community → | I want | to live | near people with similar interests. | YES |
| ex. refrigerator → | I want | to have | a large refrigerator. | NO |
| | I want | to+原形 | | |

**Your sentence:**    I want _____

**PATTERN 3** 「自分にとって～が大切だから」

| ex. environment → | The environment | is important | to me. | | YES |
| ex. hobby → | My figures | are important | to me. | I need space to keep them. | NO |
| | 大切な物 | be 動詞+important | to me | | |

**Your sentence:** _____ important to me.

**More sentences:** _____

_____

_____

**7.** 新しいメンバーとグループになって、もう一度考えを共有しましょう。自分の意見をより分かりやすく説明することができますか？

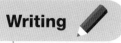

5

# 良い辞書を使いましょう

"figure"といえば机に置くキャラクターのフィギュアのことを考えますが、英語ではそれ以外の意味もたくさんあります。

- As we can see in <u>figure</u> 8, people are retiring early. (図)
- He is a prominent <u>figure</u> in politics these days. (人物)
- It took him a long time to <u>figure</u> the answer. (計算する)
- A dark <u>figure</u> was seen walking in the garden. (姿)
- What are the unemployment <u>figures</u> for last year? (数値)
- The girl's father <u>figured</u> a lot in the story. (登場する)

英文を読む際に、1つしか意味が表示されない翻訳アプリを使うと、文中の意味とは異なる意味で表示される可能性があります。無料アプリよりも有料アプリ、有料アプリよりも電子辞書、電子辞書よりも紙の辞書の方が、多くの意味が記載されています。"figure"の場合も、紙の辞書では**右の写真のように**たくさんの意味が載っています。あなたが使用している辞書でも、同じぐらいの意味が出てくるか確認しましょう。

初めて調べる英単語は、もちろん良い辞書を使用することが重要です。しかし、よく知っている英単語でも、調べた方が良い時もあります。

| fork | （名詞）フォーク |
| | （動詞）二つに別れる |
| foot | （名詞）足 |
| | （動詞）払う |

英単語は全部知っているのにも関わらず、文章の意味が理解できない時は、その英単語はあなたがまだ知らない意味として、文章中で使われているかもしれません。よく知っている英単語も、辞書を使って調べてみましょう。

出典：（株）大修館書店『ジーニアス英和辞典〈改訂版〉』(1994)

下線部の意味を選択してください。選択肢は全て、辞書に載っている下線部の英単語の意味です。

1. They drew water from the <u>spring</u>.
　　　a. 春　　b. 泉　　c. ばね　　d. 急に…になる　　e. 提案を急に持ち出す

2. I'm sorry, we don't <u>carry</u> umbrellas.
　　　a. 運ぶ　　b. 伝える　　c. 掲載する　　d. 扱っている　　e. 可決する

# Unit 2  Faberge Eggs

## Conversation Box:

❖ Have you ever heard of Faberge eggs?

❖ What was the gift that was most important to you?

## Do you know these words?

すでに知っている単語の□にチェック印✓を書いて、下の意味と線で結びましょう。なお、分からない単語があれば辞書を使って、全ての単語を線で結びましょう。

□ imperial      □ ornament      □ decorate      □ range      □ remain

● the area covered   ● something that adds beauty   ● stay   ● add an ornament to something   ● relating to an emperor

# Faberge Eggs

You may have heard of Faberge eggs in movies and television series. As gorgeous and extremely rare items, they have been used in the plots of productions that range from children's cartoons to James Bond films. Often they are the object of an elaborate heist. But originally, these ornamental eggs were given as gifts among the imperial family of Russia.                                                                5

The House of Faberge was a jewelry maker that started in 1842 in Saint Petersburg. The company became known for its quality, and in 1885 Russian Tsar Alexander III asked them to create an egg-shaped ornament as a gift for his wife. Faberge made an egg that opened up. Inside was a golden yolk and a golden hen. Inside the golden hen was a diamond crown and a ruby pendant.    10
Alexander and his wife were so pleased that Faberge was named the official jeweler of the Imperial Court. Every year from then on, he produced decorative eggs as gifts for the wives and mothers of Russian tsars.

The reason for the egg shape was that the present was for Easter. Eggs have long been associated with Easter, and have been decorated as a symbol of new   15
life. In some countries, eggs are emptied before making delicate designs on them. In others, eggs are boiled and children paint them. Then games are played with them, such as hiding and then finding the eggs.

The Faberge eggs, though, were ornaments made with gold and jewels. Each was unique, and held a surprise ornament inside. They were also   20
important to the imperial family because they celebrated people and events in their lives. The Alexander Palace Egg was a green egg that had the portraits of cach of the family's children. Inside was a miniature of their favorite home. When the Trans-Siberian railway was completed, an egg with the map of the railway was made. Inside was a miniature train that actually moved. The   25
Faberge eggs that remain today are each valued for their view into history as well as their craftsmanship and splendor.

## Words

| | | |
|---|---|---|
| gorgeous 豪華な | cartoon 子供向けアニメ | elaborate 精巧な、手の込んだ |
| heist 強盗 | tsar 皇帝 | yolk 卵黄 | Easter 復活祭 | portrait 肖像画 |

8

## Comprehension

1. Alexander III chose the House of Faberge to make the first egg because _____.
    a. Faberge was the official jeweler of the Imperial Court
    b. Faberge was known as a high quality jeweler
    c. Only Faberge made egg ornaments

2. Write T for True, or F for False.
    _____ The tsar was pleased with the first Faberge egg.
    _____ The first Faberge egg was for Easter, but then they were given for other celebrations.
    _____ Faberge started the tradition of decorating eggs for Easter.

3. Why were the Faberge eggs important to the imperial family?
    They were _____, and they _____ the family.

4. Why are Faberge eggs valuable today?
    They are _____, and they show us some _____.

5. How much do you think the original Faberge eggs cost today? _____
    Check the internet for news of the auction of a Faberge egg in recent history. What was the price?

    _____

## Vocabulary Focus

| **associate** | core meaning:<br>連想する | （動）連想する、…と結びつけて考える |
| --- | --- | --- |
| | | （動）仲間に加える |
| association（協会、組合）も associate から来ます。 | | （動）交際する |
| | | （動）共同で行う |
| 「サッカー」は Association Football の省略から来ました。 | | （名）仲間、同僚 |
| | | （名）準会員 |

associate または association を適切な形にして以下の文を完成させましょう。

1. He doesn't like to _____ with people who lie.
2. We joined an _____ that helps people in need.
3. Black cats are _____ with Halloween and bad luck.
4. I like my job because I have some great business _____.
5. My father is an _____ professor.

9

## Thinking about the Topic

Prized possessionは自分にとって一番大切なものです。自分のprized possessionを紹介して
みましょう。

**1.** 自分の大切なものをいくつか考えてみましょう：

その中から一つ選んで○で囲んでください。

**2.** 選んだものについての様子は：

大きさ：　○ big　　○ small

重さ：　　○ heavy　○ light

色：　　_____

素材：　_____

○ old　　○ new
○ round　○ square
その他：

_____

_____

_____

**3.** 自分にとって大切である理由：

 **Writing**

Topic: What is your prized possession?

**4.** 自分の prized possession を英語にしましょう：

My prized possession is a _____.

**5.** prized possession を描写しましょう：

| PATTERN 1 | It is ＋形容詞、色 |

| PATTERN 2 | It has ＋もの |
    ex.    It has three pockets.
    ex.    It has a picture of Mickey Mouse on it.

| PATTERN 3 | It is made of ＋素材 |

> 当たり前の情報を書かなくてもOK! 例えば、本だったらIt's made of paper. は必要ありません。

**Your sentences**: _____

_____

_____

_____

**6.** 大切である理由を英語にしてみましょう：

It's important to me because...
- [人] gave it to me.
- It reminds me of [思い出す場所、時期など].
- I use it every day.
- It's my favorite.

**Your sentence**:

_____

**7.** あなたの prized possession が何かを言わずに発表して、クラスメートが当てられるか試してみましょう。

2

Faberge Eggs

## 品詞を意識しましょう

文章の理解が難しい時は、単語の品詞が原因の場合もあります。よく知っている単語がいつもと違う品詞で使われていることに気が付かないと、文章の意味を理解することが出来ません。

- ・Please <u>pen</u> in an answer to the questions.　　×ペン　〇ペンで記入する
- ・A whale has <u>beached</u> nearby.　　　　　　　　×浜　〇浜に乗り上げる

単語の品詞を判断するには、以下のヒントを使いましょう。
例文はplanを使っています：

## plan　　　　plan

(名) = 予定、計画　　(動) = 計画を立てる、…するつもりである

1. 単語の前にa, the, myや数字があるときは：**名詞**
   This is <u>a</u> good plan.　　　　　　Do you like <u>my</u> plan?
2. -edがついていると動詞だが、-ingなら**動詞**または**動名詞**。
   We are planning a party.（**動詞**）　I am not good at party planning.（**動名詞**）
3. 助動詞（can, could, will, mayなど）が単語の前にあるときは：**動詞**
   I <u>will</u> plan for that in my report.　She <u>cannot</u> plan the event without help.
4. 否定の場合、notは動詞と使い、noは名詞と使う。
   He did <u>not</u> plan for that.（**動詞**）　I have <u>no</u> plans for tonight.（**名詞**）
5. -sがついている単語は複数形の**名詞**または**動詞**なので、-sだけでは判断できない。
   She plan<u>s</u> good parties.（**動詞**）　Her plan<u>s</u> are good.（**名詞**）
6. 命令形がわかりにくいときもある。文頭にある場合は要注意。
   <u>Plan</u> for it!（命令形で**動詞**）　　<u>Plans</u> were made.（複数形の**名詞**、受動態）

初めて見る単語も、品詞を把握した上で意味を調べると、どの意味で使用されているのか判断がしやすくなります。

**Let's Try!**　下線部の単語の品詞を書きなさい。
1. We <u>booked</u> a room at a famous hotel in Italy.　Book　= ＿＿＿＿＿
2. I gave her a <u>ride</u> home from the station.　　　Ride　= ＿＿＿＿＿
3. The missiles can <u>home</u> in on a target from miles away.
   　　　　　　　　　　　　　　　　　　　　　　　　Home = ＿＿＿＿＿
5. They <u>milked</u> their kind uncle for all he could give them.
   　　　　　　　　　　　　　　　　　　　　　　　　Milk　= ＿＿＿＿＿

### Conversation Box:

- ❖ Do you have a part-time job? If not, do you want one?
- ❖ Would you like a part-time job related to animals?

## Do you know these words?

すでに知っている単語の□にチェック印✓を書いて、下の意味と線で結びましょう。なお、分からない単語があれば辞書を使って、全ての単語を線で結びましょう。

□ app       □ client       □ flexible       □ first aid       □ interfere

● 依頼人、顧客   ● 妨げとなる、   ● アプリ   ● 救急手当   ● 融通の利く
　　　　　　　　　　邪魔になる

# Dog Walkers

🎧 10 As a college student, what kinds of jobs do you think of when looking for a part-time job – food service or retail? How about walking dogs? Dog walking is a job that has appeared in many of the world's biggest cities. These are places where very wealthy people live within walking distance of college campuses. People in exclusive neighborhoods need people 5 to walk their dogs for them, and college students need flexible jobs that do not interfere with their classes. New York is particularly designed in this way – with the upscale East Side near to colleges and student housing.

🎧 11 New York was actually one of the first places to have professional dog walkers. A man named Jim Buck is famous for starting a dog walking service 10 in 1960. He quit his job as salesman to follow his dream of making dog walking a career. His slim well-dressed figure walking with five or six dogs was well known in Manhattan. Soon he was walking 30 to 40 dogs every day. In the end, his dog walking company had 24 employees and walked over 150 dogs every day. 15

🎧 12 Now there are many dog walking agencies in New York, some started by former employees of Jim Buck. They offer a variety of services, and recently have added GPS tracking, phone apps, and blogs. Not everyone can become a dog walker – qualifications such as animal first aid are required, and applicants must pass interviews. Clients want dog walkers to be punctual, and 20 to understand the needs of their dogs.

🎧 13 Walking dogs as a job sounds easy, but there are many challenges. You have to know a lot about dogs, and also about the dog walking laws in your city. You also have to arrive on time every day no matter the weather. Some dogs are cooperative, but some are challenging. Some clients are challenging, too! 25 On the other hand, it's a great way to get exercise, and you get to become close to a variety of dogs. If you love dogs, this might be the dream job for you.

## Words

retail 小売店　　exclusive 高級な　　upscale 高級な　　slim ほっそりした

qualification 資格　　applicant 志願者　　punctual 時間を守る

## Comprehension

1. What set the stage for dog walking as a part-time job?

   People who live in _____ want to own dogs, but they don't have time
   to _____ them. Students need jobs that fit their _____.

2. Was Jim Buck's dog walking company successful?

   _____

3. What kind of people can't get a job as a dog walker? Think of a few types of people.
   - People who _____
   - People who _____

4. What rules are there in your town for dog walking? Research on the internet.
   - Dog walkers must _____
   - Dog walkers must not _____

5. Write T for True, or F for False.

   _____ Jim Buck was the first person to walk other people's dogs for money.

   _____ Dog walking agencies have changed their services with the times.

   _____ There are probably a lot of people who hire dog walkers in New York.

   _____ Jobs as a dog walker are probably available in other cities, too.

## Vocabulary Focus

| challenge | core meaning:<br>挑む | （名）やりがいのあること、難しい問題 |
| --- | --- | --- |
| | | （名）挑戦 |
| 日本語の「チャレンジする」は英語だと try, attempt になる。英語の challenge の目的語は通常は人にしか使えない。 | | （名）疑い |
| | | （動）いどむ、挑戦する |
| | | （動）異議を唱える、疑う |

それぞれの文の challenge の意味を選択肢から選びましょう。

1. ____ The group challenged the court's decision.
2. ____ I accepted his challenge to another match.
3. ____ Global warming is the biggest challenge of our generation.
4. ____ The bully challenged him to try a dangerous stunt.
5. ____ I would prefer a job that has challenge.

| |
| --- |
| A. やりがいのあること |
| B. 難しい問題 |
| C. 挑戦 |
| D. いどむ |
| E. 異議を唱える |

**1.** できるだけ多くのアルバイトを書いてみましょう。

| Part-time Jobs for Students |
| --- |
|  |

**2.** 上記から3つのアルバイトを選んで、その仕事の良い点と悪い点を考えましょう。

Part-time Job 1: _____

| Good Points | Bad Points |
| --- | --- |
|  |  |

Part-time Job 2: _____

| Good Points | Bad Points |
| --- | --- |
|  |  |

Part-time Job 3: _____

| Good Points | Bad Points |
| --- | --- |
|  |  |

# Writing

**Topic: Give the good and bad points of a part-time job.**

**3.** 2からアルバイトを1つ選んでください: _____

**4.** 良い点と悪い点を、以下のパターンを使って英語で書いてみましょう。

Good / Bad

| PATTERN 1 | 「～をしないといけない」（悪い点として） |

ex. | You | have to | stand | for many hours. | BAD
ex. | You | have to | smile | even when customers are rude. | BAD

You　　　 have to　 原型の動詞
（その仕事をする人は）

**Your sentence**: You _____

| PATTERN 2 | 「～をすることができる」（良い点として） |

ex. | You | get to | wear | a cute uniform. | GOOD
ex. | You | get to | listen | to music. | GOOD

You　　　 get to　　 原型の動詞

**Your sentence**: You _____

| PATTERN 3 | 「～をすることができる・できない」（許可、可能性） |

ex. | You | can | buy | items at a discount price. | GOOD
ex. | You | can't | dye | your hair. | BAD

You　　 can/can't 原型の動詞

**Your sentence**: You _____

**Other sentences**:

The salary is good.　　　　　　　It's tiring.

The atmosphere is good.　　　　　It's a popular shop.

**More sentences**: _____

_____

_____

**5.** グループで一人ずつ発表してから、どれが一番良いアルバイトか議論しましょう。

3

Dog Walkers

## 日本語と英語の違い①：主語

英語で文章を書く際に主語で困ることがありますが、日本語との文法の違いをよく考えると分かりやすくなります。まずは、英語の主語は日本語の文の「は」や「が」がついている名詞とイコールになると考えてはいけません。

私は財布を盗まれた。　　　≠　　I was …

└── 「私」は動作者（財布を盗んだ人）でも
盗まれた物（財布）でもない

「私は」はトピックを示している：

私は　　　財布を盗まれた。 ＝　My wallet was stolen.

└── 「私」に関して、
「私」といえば…

└── 英語にはトピックを伝える位置がない。しかし、Myがあるので自分に起こったことが分かる

今日は　　　天気がいい。　　≠　　Today is …

　　　　　　　　　　　　　　 ＝　The weather is great today.

└── 「今日に関して」…

└── 副詞としてトピックを入れることがある

「私は」「今日は」が動作者でない時は、省略できる場合が多い：

私は財布を盗まれた。　　　今日は天気がいい。

英語の場合、文は主語中心的にできている。

　能動態では主語が実際に動作をする　　受動態では主語は動作をされたもの
　 I like movies. 　　　　　　　　　　 My wallet was stolen.

上記のように、英語の主語を書く時は、日本語の文の「は」についている名詞を使うのではなく、動作者から考えると分かりやすくなるでしょう。

**Let's Try!**

1. 私は財布が空っぽだ。　_____ is empty.
2. 私は先生に褒められた。　_____ was praised by _____.

# The Navaho Indians

### Conversation Box:

❖ What indigenous peoples around the world do you know?

❖ What foreign manners and customs do you know?

❖ Do you know Japanese customs well?

## Do you know these words?

すでに知っている単語の□にチェック印✓を書いて、下の意味と線で結びましょう。なお、分からない単語があれば辞書を使って、全ての単語を線で結びましょう。

□ tribe   □ significant   □ taboo   □ plentiful   □ preserve

● 重要   ● 保護する   ● たっぷりの   ● 禁忌   ● 部族

# The Navaho Indians

What has happened to the people who lived in the Americas before the Europeans arrived? In the case of the United States, 574 tribes currently live on what are called reservations. These are areas designated for the tribes, where they have their own government, laws, and police. Each tribe has its own unique culture and lifestyle.

The largest reservation is that of the Navaho Indians. The Navaho Indians have herded sheep, goats, and horses on this high-altitude desert land, and are known for their beautifully weaved rugs and intricate religion. It is also significant that the Navaho language is still spoken throughout the reservation. Many other tribes have switched to speaking mainly English.

Navaho manners and customs are vastly different from those of American culture, and this sometimes causes misunderstandings. For example, it is taboo to look directly at someone when talking to them, while eye contact is important in American society. Furthermore, Navahos don't greet each other when they meet, even between good friends. If you visit someone's home, you shouldn't knock on the door as soon as you arrive. Rather, wait in your car for a while first. This custom comes from their religious beliefs. If one enters as soon as they arrive, ghosts will come in with them.

While these customs may seem cold or distant, the Navaho have a strong sense of hospitality. They always offer plentiful food and drink to visitors. They are also known to help anyone in need, or take in children who need a home. The society is unique, as well. It is matriarchal, which means that the woman is the head of the family. When married, the husband enters the family of the wife. If a woman wants a divorce, she merely leaves her husband's belongings outside the door. That signals that he is no longer welcome.

Native American tribes continue to face problems with the American government and in living together with the surrounding American culture. We need to do what we can to preserve living cultures such as those of native Americans.

## Words

reservation 特別保留地　　designate 指定する　　herd 集めて移動させる家畜の飼い方

high-altitude 高地　weave 織る　rug 敷物　intricate 複雑な　matriarchal 女家長制

## Comprehension

1. Search the internet for some other Native American tribes.

_____    _____

_____    _____

2. Think of a situation where differences between American and Navaho cultures might cause trouble. _____

_____

3. Which is not different between Navaho and American cultures?
   a. language
   b. communication manners
   c. hospitality
   d. family structure

4. Write T for True, or F for False.

   _____ Many other tribes didn't have their own languages.

   _____ Some Navajo customs come from their religion.

   _____ Not greeting a friend is unusual in American culture.

   _____ In Navaho culture, women have more power than men.

## Vocabulary Focus

| leave<br>core meaning:<br>去る | | （動）去る、出発する |
| --- | --- | --- |
| | | （動）退職する、退学する、卒業する、家出する |
| leave alone, leave go, leave off など leave を含む表現は多くある。<br>leafの複数形（leaves）も同じスペルと発音になっている。 | | （動）置き忘れる、置いていく、預ける |
| | | （動）…のままにしておく |
| | | （名）休暇、許可 |

それぞれの文のleaveの意味を選択肢から選びましょう。

1. ____ <u>Leave</u> your bags with the front desk clerk.
2. ____ I'd like to take a short <u>leave</u> to deal with a family issue.
3. ____ I lived in Chicago after <u>leaving</u> school.
4. ____ I <u>left</u> my umbrella in the train!
5. ____ Don't <u>leave</u> the windows open all day.
6. ____ He <u>left</u> his hometown to find a better job elsewhere.

| A. 去る |
| --- |
| B. 卒業する |
| C. 置き忘れる |
| D. 預ける |
| E. …のままにしておく |
| F. 休暇 |

21

## Thinking about the Topic

1. 日本のマナーや習慣をできるだけたくさん考えてみましょう。

| At Home | As a Guest |
|---|---|
| 例）take off shoes before entering | |

| Hospitality | Manners when Eating |
|---|---|
| | 例）hold rice bowl with left hand |

2. リーディングパッセージから、ナバホ族のマナーと習慣をリストアップしましょう。

**Navaho Customs**

例）do not speak when meeting a friend

日本と同じものに○、日本と違う物に×をつけましょう。

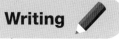

## Writing

**Topic: Compare Japanese manners to those of other countries.**

**3.** 日本のマナーや習慣を以下のパターンを使って完全文で書いてみましょう。

| PATTERN 1 | | 「人は（普段）～をする」 | | |
|---|---|---|---|---|
| ex. | Japanese people | take off | their shoes | when entering a home. HOME |
| ex. | Hosts | offer | a lot of food | to guests. HOST |
| | する人（複数形） | 現在形 | 複数形 | |

**Your sentence:**   Japanese people _____

| PATTERN 2 | | 「～をすることが礼儀正しい」 | | |
|---|---|---|---|---|
| ex. | | It is polite | to hold | the rice bowl with your left hand. EAT |
| ex. | When visiting, | it is polite | to bring | a gift. GUEST |
| | | it is polite | to + 原形 | |

**Your sentence:**   It is polite _____

| PATTERN 3 | | 「～すべきだ」 | | |
|---|---|---|---|---|
| ex. | You | should | arrive | early. GUEST |
| ex. | A host | should | prepare | slippers for guests to use. HOST |
| | する人 | should | 原形 | |

**Your sentence:**   You _____

**4.** グループで書いた文を比べましょう。日本のマナーについての考えは同じですか？

**5.** 以下の海外の習慣の中から1つ選んで、日本と比較する文を書いてみましょう。

| 海外のマナー | ● some countries have a custom of being "fashionably late"<br>● America: hosts prepare special towels for guests<br>● Europe and America: shouldn't touch the dishes while eating<br>● India: shouldn't use your left hand to eat |
|---|---|

例）In many countries people shake hands when they meet, but Japanese people bow.

_____

_____

ナバホ族と日本の似ているところについて、以下の文を完成させましょう。

In both the Navaho and Japanese cultures, _____

**4**

The Navaho Indians

23

*Writing Focus*

## 日本語と英語の違い②：動詞

英語で文章を書く際に、もう一つ困ることは動詞です。日本語との大きな違いの一つは、英語は名詞ベースではなく動詞ベースだということです。

日本語でよくあるパターンは「名詞+する」：

食事する　　　　電話する　　　　スキーする　　　　就職活動する

英語の場合、同じ概念を表している動詞と名詞は3つのパターンがあります：

| 同じ単語が名詞・動詞両方として使われる | 名詞は動詞からできた新しい形の単語 | 名詞は動詞の動名詞と不定詞の形を使う |
|---|---|---|
| ski (スキー板、スキーをする)<br>iron（アイロン、アイロンをかける） | information: inform (伝える) + ation<br>decision: decide (決める) から | run (走ることはrunning, to run)<br>swim (泳ぐことはswimming, to swim) |
| **動詞として使う際は単語をそのまま使う** | **元の動詞を使うと良い** | **元の動詞を使う** |
| × We did skiing last weekend.<br>○ We skied last weekend. | △ We gave information about the event to him.<br>○ We informed him about the event. | × We did swimming.<br>○ We swam. |

日本語で使われている外来語を英語にする時は、特に気をつけないといけません。

日本語では「+する」と使われていても、英語だと「+ do」ではないことが多くあります。

「海外でハイキングをした」　　×　I did hiking abroad.
　　　　　　　　　　　　　　　○　I hiked abroad.
　　　　　　　　　　　　　　　○　I went hiking abroad.

知らない英語を調べる時も気をつけましょう。たとえば「消毒する」と書きたい時に、「消毒 (disinfection)」を調べてdoを付けて使うと、おかしな英語になってしまいます。「消毒する」を検索すると、動詞のdisinfectが出てくるので、動詞として調べると良いでしょう。

 **Let's Try!**
1. 父は毎朝ジョギングします。　My father ＿＿＿＿＿＿＿ every morning.
2. 腸は栄養素を吸収します。　The intestines ＿＿＿＿＿＿＿ nutrients.

24

# Unit 5 — Hans, the Talking Horse

Das lesende und rechnende Pferd, mit seinem Lehrer HERRN von OSTEN (Berlin)

## Conversation Box:

❖ What animals have humans tried to communicate with?

❖ Have you heard the story of Clever Hans?

## Do you know these words?

すでに知っている単語の□にチェック印✓を書いて、下の質問に答えてみましょう。必要な場合は辞書を使ってください。

□ interact    □ react          □ handler          □ suspicious    □ prejudice

Which one...
● happens between two people
● happens to one person

handle means うまく扱う、操る.
Can you imagine what this person's job is?

Which one...
● is an opinion from before
● is the result of the other

# Hans, the Talking Horse

19     In 1904, big news spread through Europe, then around the world: a horse had been trained to talk! This interested both the general public as well as serious scientists. Can horses and maybe other animals learn to communicate with humans? It seemed like a dream come true.

20     This horse, named Hans, used his foot to communicate. He stomped in a 5 certain pattern for each letter of the alphabet. Spelling that way, he could answer any question. His owner, Wilhelm von Osten, was a retired math teacher. After teaching children his whole life, he believed that he could also teach a horse. He spent hours and hours together with the horse. Hans could answer questions about the calendar, understand a clock, and even read. 10

21     Researchers of various specialties came to test this horse, but it seemed that the horse was actually communicating. Finally, one psychologist found that if Hans could not see his owner, he could not answer the questions. Von Osten was not giving the horse secret cues as a trick, though. He really believed that Hans could talk and think. Actually, Hans had learned to read human body 15 language. Von Osten's body changed in very small ways, and this signaled to Hans when to stomp his foot.

22     This is now called the Clever Hans Effect. When training animals, our bodies send signals without our knowledge. The animals are watching us carefully, and use these signals to interact with us. Sometimes this can have 20 dangerous results. For example, dogs searching for drugs and bombs were found to react differently if their handler thought a bag was suspicious. We expect dogs to search for these items only by smell, but they are also being affected by the prejudices of their handlers.

23     Although we cannot communicate with horses by teaching them the 25 alphabet, we did learn that we are communicating with animals through our body language. Perhaps we can communicate better with animals if we are aware of the signals that we are sending.

## Words

| | | |
|---|---|---|
| stomp 足を強く踏み鳴らす | psychologist 心理学者 | cue 合図、ヒント |

## Comprehension

1. When Hans couldn't see his owner, he couldn't answer the questions because _____.
   a. von Osten was showing Hans the answers secretly
   b. Hans was lonely
   c. Hans was stubborn
   d. Hans needed von Osten's body language to know when to stomp

2. In the end, was Hans really understanding the questions? _____

3. What do you think von Osten's reaction was to the report that Hans couldn't really talk and think? _____ Check the internet and find out what von Osten did after the testing finished: _____

   _____

4. Write T for True, or F for False.
   _____ The horse answered all questions by stomping his foot.
   _____ It wasn't easy for von Osten to teach the horse all of the information.
   _____ Hans could understand von Osten's voice but not written words.
   _____ Now, we all know these signals and use them to train animals.

## Vocabulary Focus

| **signal** | core meaning:<br>信号 | （名）信号、合図 |
| --- | --- | --- |
| | | （名）兆候、きざし |
| 動詞の使い方：signal [意味] to [相手]、signal [人] to [してほしい 動作]、signal that [伝えたいこと] | | （動）合図する |

それぞれの英語の表現と対応する意味を線で結びましょう。

traffic signal ●           ● 警報

hand signal ●           ● 踏切の信号

warning signal ●           ● 交通信号

smoke signal ●           ● のろし

railway signal ●           ● 手信号

**1.** 例のように、パッセージの中に登場する人物が考えたこと、言ったことを整理しましょう。

**（例）Paragraph 1**

| 人物 | 思ったこと |
|---|---|
| people around the world | ● a horse could talk with humans<br>● maybe animals can communicate with humans |

**Paragraph 2**

| 人物 | やりたかったこと |
|---|---|
| ① Wilhelm von Osten | |

**Paragraph 3**

| 人物 | できなかったこと |
|---|---|
| ② Hans | |

| 人物 | できたこと |
|---|---|
| ③ Hans | |

| 人物 | 信じていたこと |
|---|---|
| ④ | ● Hans understood his questions<br>● Hans was really answering the questions |

**Paragraph 4-5**

| 人物 | よく見ているもの |
|---|---|
| ⑤ Animals being trained by humans | |

| 人物 | 分かったこと |
|---|---|
| ⑥ We | |

**Writing** Topic: Briefly explain the passage.

2. 例にならって、1で準備した情報を文にしましょう。複数のアイディアがあるところは、
   一つだけ選んで使いましょう。

（例）Paragraph 1

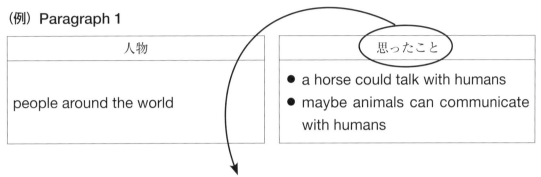

| 人物 | 思ったこと |
|---|---|
| people around the world | ● a horse could talk with humans<br>● maybe animals can communicate with humans |

People around the world <u>thought that</u> a horse could talk with humans.

① _____

② _____

③ _____

④ _____

⑤ _____

⑥ _____

3. 書いた文を以下の型に入れて、パッセージの要約になるか確認してみましょう。

（例） After retiring from teaching, ①. After training, his horse ②, but ③. ④.
Actually, ⑤. From this story, ⑥.

## *Writing Focus* — 英語の句読点

英語の句読点を正しく書きましょう。

1. 日本語の句読点を使わないようにする。

   英語の句読点: . , ! ? " " ' ' : ;
   日本の句読点: 。 、「 」～ … 『 』 ・

2. 手書きの際に、ピリオド ( . ) とコンマ ( , ) の形に注意する。

   ● ピリオドは、線ではなく、点で書く。
   ● ピリオドは、紙をペン先で打つのではなく、きちんと見える点を書く。
   ● コンマは、左にカーブさせる。日本語のカンマのように右に伸ばさない。

   例:

   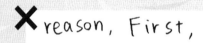     

   ↑ピリオドとコンマの区別ができない      ↑日本語の句読点

3. 句読点は単語のすぐ後に置く。句読点の後はスペースを一文字分空けてから次の単語を始める。ワープロの時はスペース、手書きの時は文字と句読点の位置に気を付ける。

   I went to the store ,then to the station . Then, I took a train !

   I went to the store, then to the station. Then, I took a train!

**Let's Try!**   ミスの種類を a, b, c の中から選択しましょう。

a. 英語の句読点ではない    b. 句読点の形    c. 句読点の位置

# Unit 6  Jacinda Ardern

## Conversation Box:

❖ Do you know Jacinda Ardern?
❖ What is she famous for?

### Do you know these words?

すでに知っている単語の□にチェック印✓を書いて、下の意味と線で結びましょう。なお、分からない単語があれば辞書を使って、全ての単語を線で結びましょう。

☐ compassion     ☐ immigrant     ☐ impact     ☐ restriction     ☐ reassure

● a major      ● calm someone's    ● a person coming to   ● a limitation    ● understanding
  effect         worries         live from abroad        others' pain

# Jacinda Ardern

🎧 24
New Zealand's 40th Prime Minister, Jacinda Ardern is known not only for her strong and successful responses to crises that have rocked her country, but for her compassion and friendly nature. Jacinda spent her childhood in a small town. Her father was a police officer. There were many children in this town without enough food, and this encouraged her to enter politics. From the age of 17 she was active in a political party. 5

🎧 25
In politics, Jacinda was originally known for her youth. She became prime minister of New Zealand at the age of 37, one of the youngest world leaders. She was the second leader to have a baby while in office, and the first head of state to bring a baby to the floor of the United Nations. Leading up to her 10 election, New Zealand was in a state of "Jacindamania" – she performed as a DJ, and her partner was a famous television personality.

🎧 26
But Jacinda was more than just attractive. As prime minister, she kept New Zealand safe during a particularly challenging time. In 2019, two mosques were attacked by an anti-immigrant terrorist, and 50 people were killed. Many 15 people in New Zealand owned guns, but nevertheless within a month of the incident, her government was able to ban ownership of semi-automatic weapons. Then when the coronavirus pandemic struck, she used the strategy of "go hard and go early" – New Zealand was the first to close ports of entry to foreigners, and had a strict lockdown. This had a heavy impact on the 20 economy, but New Zealand was quick to see the coronavirus disappear. They could then return to a normal lifestyle, while keeping basic coronavirus measures in place.

🎧 27
While acting as prime minister, though, she still keeps a warm and friendly demeanor. Many call her by her first name, Jacinda, and she stops to talk with 25 the people she meets when driving or shopping. When announcing coronavirus restrictions, she reassured children that the Tooth Fairy and Easter Bunny would be allowed to continue their jobs – two mythical figures that children believe in. Jacinda Ardern shows a good balance of leadership and kindness. 30

## Words

mosque モスク、イスラム教寺院     semi-automatic 半自動の

port of entry 出[入]国港     demeanor 態度     mythical 神話上の、想像上の

## Comprehension

1. Jacinda originally wanted to join politics to _____ .
   a. keep laws strict
   b. help people
   c. promote the female viewpoint

2. What is the meaning of "have" in this sentence:
   "She was the second leader to have a baby while in office."
      a. 出産する      b. ～がいる      c. 連れてくる

3. How old is this baby now? Search on the internet: _____ years old

4. In what two ways did she keep New Zealand safe?
   She _____ semi-automatic weapons, and she _____ the coronavirus disappear quickly.

5. Write T for True, or F for False.
   _____ Jacinda was very popular when she first became prime minister.
   _____ There were no disadvantages to Jacinda's coronavirus policy.

## Vocabulary Focus

| strike | core meaning:<br>打つ | （動）打つ、たたく、殴る |
|---|---|---|
| | | （動）ぶつかる、突き当たる |
| （名）：ストライキ、ストライク、攻撃<br><br>過去形：struck<br><br>名詞のstroke（一打）もstrikeから来ます | | （動）[病気、災害]…を不意に襲う |
| | | （動）心に浮かぶ、心を打つ |
| | | （動）鳴らす、弾く |
| | | （動）削除する |
| | | （動）ストライキをする |

strikeを適切な形にして以下の文を完成させましょう。

1. Cinderella must go home before the clock _____ twelve.
2. They _____ his name from the list.
3. The earthquake _____ our city on that day.
4. The workers are _____ for better pay.
5. Without the brakes on, the car rolled down the street and _____ a tree.

## Thinking about the Topic

1. 思いつく有名人をできるだけ書いてみましょう。

| Historical People: | Authors, Directors, Artists: | Entertainers, Musicians, Actors: |
|---|---|---|
|  |  |  |

2. 調べてみたい人を選んで、以下のことを調べてメモをとりましょう。

Accomplishments (What are they famous for?):



Year of Birth:       Place of Birth:

University:       Major:

First Job or Main Job:

Find one strange or interesting story from their life:



What is your impression of this person?

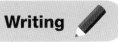

**Writing**　Topic: Introduce a famous person.

3. 調べて分かった情報を文章にまとめてみましょう。（※調べたページから文章をそのまま写さないようにしましょう）

STEP 1　まず、選んだ人は何で有名なのかを紹介します。

例） J. R. R. Tolkien is famous for writing *The Lord of the Rings* .

例） Jawaharlal Nehru was the first Prime Minister of India .

① _____

STEP 2　子供時代〜社会人までの経歴について書きます。過去のことなので、過去形を使います。

例） Stephen King was born in 1947 in Portland, Maine . He studied English at the University of Maine , then became a teacher .

② _____

_____

_____

STEP 3　ひとつ、何か面白い情報を入れましょう。

例） When J. R. R. Tolkien was a baby, he was kidnapped. But, he was returned to his family the next day.

③ _____

_____

STEP 4　調べた理由、調べてみて印象に残ったことをまとめましょう。

例） Stephen King is an inspiration because he continues to write books every year even though he is over 75 years old.

④ _____

4. 有名人の名前を言わずに②〜④を発表しましょう。聞いているグループのメンバーは、誰のことについて話しているのか予測してみましょう。

6

Jacinda Ardern

35

## 翻訳サイトの正しい使い方

英語を学習する時に、最初から機械翻訳を使ってしまうと英語力が上達しませんが、社会に出たら使う可能性があるので、正しい使い方を考えましょう。まずはサイトの弱点を理解しましょう：

1. **まだ100%は信頼できない**：機械翻訳サイトはこの数年間でずいぶん精度が上がったが、まだ誤った結果が出ることもある。

| Japanese ▼ | | English ▼ |
|---|---|---|
| 傘をさす | → ← | Point to an umbrella |

翻訳結果の英語の意味：「傘を<u>指さす</u>」

※正しい訳：open(use) an umbrella

2. **主語の問題が多い**：主語が無い日本語の文や、文の一部を翻訳サイトに入力すると、言いたいことと違う代名詞が付いたり、主語が無くてもいいのにも関わらず、入っていたりする。

右の例の場合、これが完全文だったら大丈夫なのだが、「ほうれん草が嫌いな人が多い」のような文に入れるために調べた場合は、このまま使えない。

| Japanese ▼ | | English ▼ |
|---|---|---|
| ほうれん草が嫌い | → ← | I hate spinach |

3. **文法が複雑になるほど間違いが多くなる**：少し長い文章になると、全く違う意味の英語が出てくる。この例の翻訳結果の意味は「私は、先生に助けられた生徒達を集めて、そして[誰かを]褒めた」になってしまっている。

| Japanese ▼ | | English ▼ |
|---|---|---|
| 先生が手伝ってくれた生徒を集めて褒めました | → ← | I gathered the pupils the teacher helped and praised |

**翻訳サイトを使うときの基礎**：翻訳結果を自分の使い方に合わせる必要がある。複数形、代名詞などは特に

| Japanese ▼ | | English ▼ |
|---|---|---|
| 内科の先生 | → ← | Internal medicine teacher |

注意すべきだ。そして、結果に関しては自分の判断が必要である。上の例の場合、この結果を見て「医者」と言いたいのに「教員」として出てきたことに気が付き、自分で直す必要がある。翻訳サイトは魔法のように自分の言いたいことを教えてくれるものではなく、ツールの一つにすぎない。

**Let's Try!** 翻訳サイトに、自分がよく使う日本語をいくつか入れてみましょう。正しい英語が出てきた例と、正しくない英語が出てきた例を一つずつ書いてみましょう。

Correct:

JAPANESE: _____

ENGLISH: _____

Incorrect:

JAPANESE: _____

ENGLISH: _____

# Unit 7　Color and Test Taking

## Conversation Box:

❖ Do you always do your best on tests?

❖ What helps you to concentrate?

## Do you know these words?

すでに知っている単語の□にチェック印✓を書いて、下の意味と線で結びましょう。なお、分からない単語があれば辞書を使って、全ての単語を線で結びましょう。

☐ expectation　　☐ confirm　　☐ prevent　　☐ reaction　　☐ evolutionary

● 反応　　● 防ぐ　　● 予想　　● 進化論の　　● 確認する

# Color and Test Taking

We often hear that colors can affect our moods. It's easy to see that blue walls in a room can be calming, and orange walls can make us warm and cheerful. But research has shown that colors can affect us in unusual ways, and we don't even realize it. One type of experiment in particular shows how this happens. In these experiments, people are given intellectual tests with one difference – the color of the test booklet cover. Researchers found that people did poorly when they had a test booklet with a red cover.

For example, in one experiment, an IQ test was given with the color of the test cover being red, green, or gray. Subjects whose covers were red had significantly lower scores than those with green or gray. The average results of people with green and gray covers were about the same. The researchers explained that red is a signal of danger to students. Red is often associated with failure, such as getting a lot of red pen marks on a test in school. In nature, poisonous animals and plants are often red. Seeing a red cover on the test, the subject's motivation is lowered because of an expectation of failure. As a result, the subject does in fact get a lower score.

Various other experiments have also been done to confirm these results. Avoidance is one response to danger, and prevents the person from doing their best. Some experiments were done to confirm that red triggers avoidance. In one experiment, sensors measured the body movements of test takers. When given the test booklet, those whose test had a red cover moved their bodies away from the test booklet more than those with green or grey covers.

We do not know whether reactions due to colors are evolutionary or learned. In other words, we humans may be born with certain reactions to colors, as many animals are. Or, these reactions may come from color associations that we learn throughout our lives. In either case, though, we may be being affected by colors in ways that we do not realize.

## Words

trigger 引き起こす    avoidance 回避

## Comprehension

1. The experiments introduced here _____ .

    a. are the first experiments on how colors affect us

    b. show which colors are better than others

    c. show that colors can affect us even if we don't know it

2. Write T for True, or F for False.

    _____ Students with red test booklets had lower scores than other students.

    _____ When somebody sees danger, motivation is lowered.

    _____ In an experiment, red covers did not trigger avoidance.

    _____ These experiments did not find the reason why humans react to the color red.

3. In Unit 4, "significant" meant "重要". This unit uses "significantly" for statistics, so it means _____ .

    Search the internet and find the percent usually used to show statistical significance: _____ %

4. Have you taken any tests that had red covers or red coloring? _____

    If all students have the same red cover, do you think it is fair to make an exam with a red cover? _____

    Why or why not? _____

## Vocabulary Focus

| **subject** | core meaning:<br>話題 | （名）主題、話題、テーマ |
|---|---|---|
| | | （名）科目 |
| | | （名）主語 |
| 話題、学校の科目、文法の主語、実験の被験者まで、たくさんの意味がある。<br>動詞の場合、協調が変わる：subJECT | | （名）被験者、実験動物 |
| | | （形）受けやすい、かかりやすい |
| | | （動）従属させる |
| | | （動）受けさせる、経験させる |

それぞれの文のsubjectの意味を選択肢から選びましょう。

1. _____ The American Midwest is subject to tornadoes.
2. _____ What's your favorite subject?
3. _____ The crew was subjected to bad working conditions.
4. _____ The subjects were each given the same medication.
5. _____ The verb form does not match the subject.
6. _____ I don't like talking about that. Let's change the subject.

| A. 話題 |
| B. 科目 |
| C. 主語 |
| D. 被験者 |
| E. 受けやすい |
| F. 受けさせる |

## Thinking about the Topic

リーディングパッセージでは、実験で分かったことについて学習しました。今度は、あなた自身がクラスメートにアンケートをとって、分かったことについて報告してみましょう。

1. まずは、どのようなことについてアンケートをとるか考えてみましょう。できるだけ多くのアイディアを考えてから一つに絞りましょう。面白い結果が出る話題がいいですね。

| Topic Ideas |
| --- |
|  |

アイディアの中からどれか一つ
選びましょう：

|  |
| --- |
|  |

2. 決めたテーマを英語の質問にして、3〜4つの選択肢を書いてみましょう。

Q: _____

_____

a. _____

b. _____

c. _____

d. _____

| Example |
| --- |
| **Q:** What do you drink when you are thirsty? |
| a. water |
| b. green tea |
| c. barley tea |
| d. other |

3. クラスメートにアンケートをとってみましょう。できるだけ多くの人に聞きましょう。

| choice | a. | b. | c. | d. |
| --- | --- | --- | --- | --- |
| Mark the number of people who choose each. |  |  |  |  |

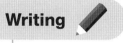

## Writing

### Topic: Report the results of a survey.

それぞれの選択肢の数字を書くだけではアンケート結果は伝わりません。大きな差や、似ているところなどを伝えましょう。

4. 集めたデータをグラフにして、以下のパターンを参考にして分析結果を説明しましょう。

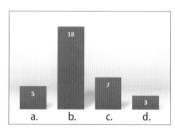

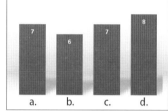

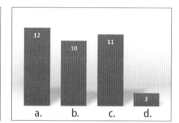

一つが他よりも多い：
Many more students
drink green tea than other
drinks.

4つとも同じぐらい：
Similar numbers of
students drink water,
green tea, barley tea, and
other drinks.

一つが他よりも少ない：
Students drink mainly
water, green tea, and
barley tea. Few drink
other drinks.

**Your Analysis:** _____

_____

_____

_____

_____

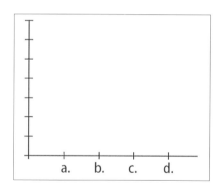

5. まとめて結果を報告しましょう。

**Step 1:** アンケートの質問と、答えた人数を書く

My question was: _____

I asked _____ university students from my English class.

**Step 2:** 上記のAnalysisを書く

_____

**Step 3:** 各選択肢の答えの数を書く

_____

**Step 4:** 自分の感想を書く

_____

## 話法の正しい書き方

高校では間接話法を学びますが、直接話法を使う機会はあまり多くありません。直接話法のルールを確認しましょう。

# Bob said, "The test was easy."

「言った」のsaid, shouted, askedなどの後には：
**カンマ + スペースを一つ**

引用符は実際に発言した言葉を囲むように置く。閉める役目の引用符も忘れずに！

発言したことの最後のピリオドは引用符の中に置く。それが全体の文のピリオドの役目にもなる。引用符の外にもピリオドを続けて置かないように注意する。

直接話法を使うとき、実際に発言した言葉をそのまま引用符の中に入れるように注意する必要がある。勝手に内容を変更したりしてはいけない。印刷したものの引用は特にそうである。例えば、元になる文章にはスペルのミスがあったとしても、そのままの状態で引用する。
レポートなどで記事からの情報をサポートとして使うときは、ほとんどのケースでは直接話法よりも間接話法の方が適切である。伝えたいのは言い方よりも情報なので、その情報を文章の中で自分の言葉にして伝えると良い。

● According to the passage, "Subjects whose covers were red had significantly lower scores than those with green or grey."

 直接話法を使う必要がない時に使うと、伝えたいことがわからない

● According to the passage, students in an experiment had significantly lower scores if their test cover was red.

 自分の伝えたいことが中心に書かれているので読みやすい

記事の強調や言い方を伝えたい場合は、直接話法を使うと良い。また、間接話法を使うときは、実際に発言した言葉をそのまま使用してはいけないので、必ず言い換えるように気を付ける。

I just love herbal tea! It's my favorite.

**Let's Try!** 右のイラストの人の言葉をそれぞれの方法で書いてみましょう。

直接話法 _____

間接話法 _____

# Unit 8　European Castles

**Conversation Box:**

❖ When you think of a castle, what kind of castle do you imagine?

❖ What stories do you know that take place in castles?

## Do you know these words?

すでに知っている単語の□にチェック印✓を書いて、下に単語の意味を書きましょう。次に分からない単語の意味を辞書で調べて書きましょう。

☐ servant　　☐ ruin　　☐ royalty　　☐ venue　　☐ aspect

_____　　_____　　_____　　_____　　_____

★パッセージを読むとき、ここで書いた意味がパッセージで使われている意味と合っているかどうかを確認しましょう。

# European Castles

32  Castles are found in the history of many countries around the world, but Europe is especially known for its castles. For one thing, there are so many of them. The number is not known exactly, but there are over 25,000. They have been built in a wide variety of styles throughout history. Secondly, many of these castles can still be used today.  5

33  Castles in Europe were built in the Middle Ages, between the 5th and 15th centuries. At this time, Europe was not divided into countries. Rather, kings ruled over areas of land. They lived in castles as a way to protect themselves and their riches. Kings who traveled through their kingdoms had castles in the places where they stayed. They brought all of their belongings and supporting  10 staff with them when moving between castles.

34  While each castle looks unique, there are some common elements. The safest place was the central tower, called the keep. This held the main headquarters as well as the living areas for the king. There was usually a great hall, a decorated room where guests were received and parties held. A  15 courtyard outside was called the bailey, where servants lived, horses were kept, and daily work was done. Slightly apart from the castle was the curtain wall. People could defend the castle from the top of the wall, and embrasures helped them to do so. These were holes or gaps in the wall from which they could shoot at enemies. Many castles also had moats, or waterways that were  20 dug out around the castle for added protection.

35  Nowadays castles can be seen all throughout Europe in various forms. Some remain only as ruins, and others have been preserved. Some offer tours or act as museums. Some are the property of current royalty, and others can be bought and sold as homes. Still others are used as venues for concerts and  25 events. Many can be rented out to hold weddings. Castles are an aspect of history that is still very much alive in Europe today.

## Words

| | | | |
|---|---|---|---|
| Middle Ages 中世 | kingdom 王国 | headquarters 本部 | courtyard 中庭 |

# Comprehension

1. Some words are explained in the passage. As in the example, find the words and underline the explanation.

> <u>A courtyard outside</u> was called the (bailey,) where servants lived, horses were kept, and daily work was done.

Do the same for these words:

| keep | great hall | embrasure | moat |
|------|-----------|-----------|------|

Can you understand these words enough from these explanations? _____

2. Choose one of these, and write a similar type of explanation

| yukata | bubble tea | Shinkansen | Doraemon | katakana |
|--------|-----------|------------|----------|----------|

3. Write T for True, or F for False.

_____ A castle's main purpose was to protect the king.

_____ Kings usually never left their castles.

_____ The king's staff lived outside of the castle.

_____ Now, all European castles are being used in some way.

# Vocabulary Focus

| **rule** | core meaning:<br><br>支配する | （名）規則、きまり |
|----------|------------------|------------------|
| | | （名）習慣、普通のこと |
| as a general rule　一般に | | （名）支配 |
| bend the rules　規則を曲げる | | （動）支配する、抑制する |
| make it a rule to do　いつも…することにしている | | （動）判決を下す |

rule を適切な形にして以下の文を完成させなさい。

1. According to the _____, players cannot touch the ball with their hands.

2. Queen Victoria _____ for 63 years.

3. When will the judge _____ on this case?

4. My uncle makes it a _____ to exercise every morning.

## Thinking about the Topic

1. 日本の城について知っていることや、調べて分かったことを書いてみましょう。

[empty box]

2. パッセージから、ヨーロッパの城について分かったことをいくつか書いて、日本の城と似ているか比較してみましょう。

| European Castles | Japanese Castles | Same? |
|---|---|---|
| 例）many have moats | have moats | ○ |
| | | |
| | | |
| | | |
| | | |
| | | |
| | | |

3. 前ページの2で集めた比較表を見て、日本の城とヨーロッパの城は「似ている」か「似ていない」かのどちらを言いたいかを決めて、パラグラフの一文目を選んでください。

   ☐   Japanese castles and European castles are similar in many ways.

   ☐   Japanese castles and European castles are different in many ways.

4. 以下のパターンを参考にして、similar を選んだ場合は○、different を選んだ場合は×の例を3つ、完全文で書きましょう。

   PATTERN FOR SIMILAR

   共通している特徴：Both castles have 複数形名詞. / Both castles are 形容詞.

   　　例：Castles in both Europe and Japan have moats .

   PATTERNS FOR DIFFERENT

   片方だけ持つ特徴：XX castles have/are ～, but YY castles do/are not.

   　　例：Japanese castles have a pyramid shape, but European castles are square.

   片方だけの例（only を使って）：Only XX castles have/are ～.

   　　例：Only European castles have a great hall for holding parties.

   比較する：XX castles are more ～ than YY castles.

   　　例：There are more European castles than Japanese castles.

   _____

   _____

   _____

5. 選んだ意見によって、以下の文でパラグラフをまとめる：

   ☐   In these ways, Japanese and European castles are very similar.

   ☐   In these ways, Japanese and European castles are quite different.

6. ルーズリーフの紙でパラグラフを書いてみましょう。ルーズリーフの書き方は次ページのコラムにあります。パラグラフの順は：

   　　3で選んだ文　→　First, Second, をつけながら4で書いた文　→　5で選んだ文

   ☆内容がほとんど決まっているので、紙での書き方に気を付けてきれいに書きましょう。

8

European Castles

**Writing Focus**

# ライティングの提出方法：手書きの場合

ワープロが登場するまではライティング課題は手書きで提出していたので、ワープロの設定は手書きの基礎からきています。まずは手書きでの正しい書き方をマスターしましょう。

**タイトル**：それぞれの単語の頭文字は大文字で書く。完全文を使わないのが普通。

左上は名前、科目名、日付を書く。日付は締切日を書く。

**段落の一行目を下げて書く：** 英語の場合は、5文字分

穴が左側になるようにしてルーズリーフを使う。

一行おきで書く

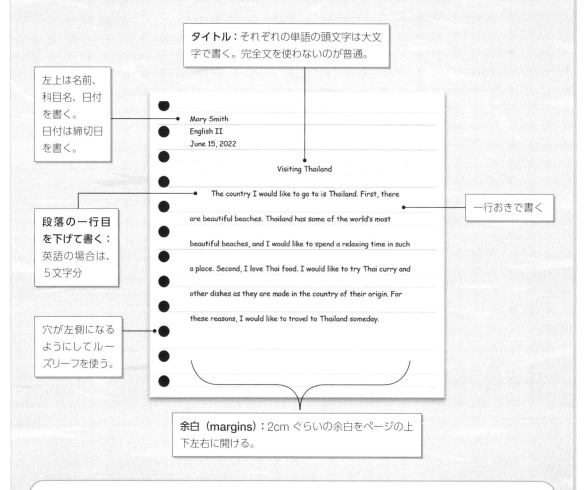

Mary Smith
English II
June 15, 2022

Visiting Thailand

　　　　The country I would like to go to is Thailand. First, there
are beautiful beaches. Thailand has some of the world's most
beautiful beaches, and I would like to spend a relaxing time in such
a place. Second, I love Thai food. I would like to try Thai curry and
other dishes as they are made in the country of their origin. For
these reasons, I would like to travel to Thailand someday.

**余白（margins）**：2cm ぐらいの余白をページの上下左右に開ける。

■**提出チェックリスト：**

☐ 書き始める前に十分に準備をする：訂正や付け足しがあるなど、完璧でなければもう一度書き直す。

☐ 英語をチェックしてから提出：自分でも確認できるようなミススペルなどの単純な間違いをしない。

☐ きれいな状態で提出：提出するまでに、折ったり曲げたりしない。また、紙を切ったり、小さくしたりせず、一枚そのまま提出する。

☐ 一般的な罫線入りのルーズリーフ紙を使う：罫線がない紙、一度別のことに使ったもの、メモ用紙などを使わない。

**Let's Try!** このフォーマットを使って、前ページで書いたパラグラフをルーズリーフに書き写してみましょう。

# Canopy Meg

**Conversation Box:**

❖ What aspect of nature were you
interested in as a child?

❖ Would you be interested in
touring a rainforest?

## Do you know these words?

すでに知っている単語の□にチェック印✓を書いて、下の意味と線で結びましょう。なお、
分からない単語があれば辞書を使って、全ての単語を線で結びましょう。

□ identify □ eventually □ observe □ attempt □ continuous

● look at ● in the end ● never stopping ● try ● find out what something is

# Canopy Meg

Dr. Margaret Lowman is known by her nickname, Canopy Meg, and for speaking out to save rainforests around the world. However, she wasn't always a strong speaker. Born in 1953, Meg was a very shy girl. She almost never spoke in school, and felt closer to nature than to other children. She loved to identify various plants that she found, and spent her days learning more about the nature around her.

This led to an active interest in science, and eventually to the rainforests in Australia, where she started her doctorate research. Until then, tree specialists had only observed trees from the ground level. They measured the tree trunks, and examined the leaves that fell to the ground. Lowman decided to attempt research on trees from within the canopy. The canopy is the very top part of the branches, where the leaves make a continuous cover. She started by making a harness to pull herself up trees. There, she found a whole new world of life. Throughout her life as a researcher, she learned many new things about trees, discovered new insects, found the reasons for trees dying, and charted the effects of global warming.

With every new discovery, Lowman was reminded of the importance of rainforests. She realized that she needed to take action where rainforests were being destroyed. Although she was very shy, this issue encouraged her to do something about it. She traveled to countries all over the world and helped the local people to find ways of using the trees without destroying them. She also built walkways in tree canopies and started canopy tourism. Not only have her efforts helped to save trees from being destroyed, but she has promoted a love for trees, canopies, nature, and science to people all over the world.

## Words

doctorate 博士号        trunk 木の幹        harness 安全ベルト、ハーネス

## Comprehension

1. Dr. Margaret Lowman was the first person to _____.
   a. study rainforests
   b. research the tops of trees
   c. chart the effects of global warming
   d. try to save rainforests

2. Complete this sentence:

   _____ and _____ are two ways that Meg accessed the tops of trees.

3. Search on "canopy tourism" on the internet. In what countries can we take canopy tours?

   _____

4. Write T for True, or F for False.

   _____ Canopy Meg had an interest in nature from a young age.

   _____ She made a new method of going up to the top of trees.

   _____ She believes that it is important to save the rainforests.

   _____ Lowman took action to save trees not only in rainforests, but all around the world.

## Vocabulary Focus

| **ground** | core meaning:<br>地面 | （名）地面、土地、土 |
|---|---|---|
| | | （名）場所、…場、[ 複数形 ] 構内 |
| grind ( 肉などをひく ) の過去形も ground で、同じスペルと発音になっている。 | | （名）話題、立場、[ 複数形 ] 根拠 |
| | | （動）地上にとどまらせる、外出を禁ずる |
| | | （動）基礎を置く、基礎を教え込む |
| | | （形）地上の、基礎の |

それぞれの文の ground の意味を選択肢から選びましょう。

| A. 土 |
|---|
| B. 構内 |
| C. 話題 |
| D. 外出を禁ずる |
| E. 基礎を置く |
| F. 基礎を教え込む |

1. ____ His theory is grounded on solid facts.
2. ____ The thief entered the grounds of the museum.
3. ____ My parents grounded me for my bad grades.
4. ____ They planted the seeds in the ground.
5. ____ The students are well grounded in the grammar rules.
6. ____ The group leader is going over the same ground that he covered yesterday.

## Thinking about the Topic

**1.** 地球を守るために私たちが出来ることについてブレーンストーミングしましょう。(SCALE)

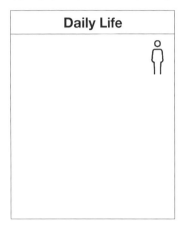

**2.** 上に書いたアイディアは、それぞれ何の助けになるか考えましょう。(ISSUES)

Keep the Environment Clean

Save Resources

Stop Species Extinction

Stop Global Warming

**3.** どのアイディアを紹介するか考えましょう。選んだアイディアに印を付けて、紹介したいアイディアをもとに、 **TYPE 1** か **TYPE 2** の形式を選んで、次のページでパラグラフを書きましょう。

1つのSCALEでできる3つのISSUES

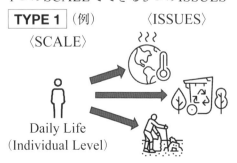

3つのSCALEでできる1つのISSUE

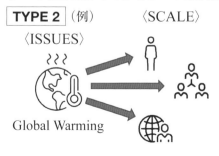

Topic: What can we do to protect the environment?

4. まずは共通したものを中心にトピックを紹介します。 TYPE 1 か TYPE 2 の形式で書きましょう。

TYPE 1                                                    SCALE
例）We can protect our environment in many ways at the individual level .

TYPE 2                    ISSUE
例）We can help stop global warming at the individual, community, and global levels.

**Your sentence**: _____

5. 選んだTYPEに合わせて、活動のアイディアを3つ紹介します。

TYPE 1
例）We can help stop global warming by using a paper fan instead of an electric fan.

TYPE 2
例）At the global level, we can join demonstrations against fossil fuels.

**Your sentences**: _____

_____

_____

6. まとめもTYPEに合わせて書きます：

TYPE 1    In this way, we all can contribute in our daily lives .

TYPE 2    In this way, there is a wide variety of things we can do to
          help stop global warming .

**Your sentence**: _____

7. パラグラフが完成したら、クラスまたはグループで発表して、生活の中でできることを考えましょう。

9

Canopy Meg

**Writing Focus**

## パラグラフの形で書きましょう

まとまった文章を書く時、それぞれのセンテンスを一行ずつ改行して書くのではなく、一つのパラグラフの形で書くようにしましょう。

> Bobby Jones is fun to spend time with.
> He has a great sense of humor.
> Once, he drew a funny picture.
> Everyone in our class laughed.

> Bobby Jones is fun to spend time with.
> He has a great sense of humor. Once, he
> drew a funny picture. Everyone in our
> class laughed.

- ✓ **手書きの場合**：次の単語を書く余裕がないと思ったところまで続けて書く。
- ✓ **ワープロの場合**：ワープロソフトは適切なところで自動的に改行するようになっているため、パラグラフが終わるまでEnterキーを使わない。

右側をぴったり揃える必要はありません。例えば、印刷物では一つの単語を二行にわたり、ハイフン（-）を使って繋げている場合もあります。しかし、それは印刷物の方法で、普段学校に提出するものには使いません。どうしても使用する必要がある時は、単語の分け方にはルールがあるので、注意しましょう。辞書に載っている音節（●のマーク）でしか区切ることは出来ません。

また、一つのパラグラフにまとめて書く課題が出た際は、英語のパラグラフは「段落」という意味なので、複数の段落に分けないように気を付けましょう。英語の段落は日本語のものより長いので、複数の段落に分けたくなるかもしれませんが、我慢しましょう。

> 　Bobby Jones is fun to spend time with.
> He has a great sense of humor, and is
> always making jokes. Once, he drew a
> funny picture of our teacher! Everyone in
> our class laughed.
> 　That's why Bobby Jones is a fun person
> to be with.

> 　Bobby Jones is fun to spend time with.
> He has a great sense of humor, and is
> always making jokes. Once, he drew a
> funny picture of our teacher! Everyone in
> our class laughed. That's why Bobby Jones
> is a fun person to be with.

前ページで準備したパラグラフを、54ページのフォーマットを使って、きれいなパラグラフの形で書いてみましょう。

54

# Dude Ranches

## Conversation Box:

❖ Have you ever ridden a horse?

❖ Do you like spending time outdoors?

## Do you know these words?

すでに知っている単語の□にチェック印✓を書いて、語根を使いながら他の単語の意味を当ててみましょう。最後に辞書で自分の書いた意味が当たっているか確認しましょう。

☐ ranch      ☐ idealize      ☐ capitalize      ☐ cattle      ☐ profitable

語根:      ideal      capital      profit

# Dude Ranches

The life of a cowboy has been idealized in American culture for a long time. Western movies capitalized on this and added to the trend. But even before movies, ranches in the American West opened up to tourism, and were popular with people who wanted a taste of ranch life. These were called dude ranches.

What exactly is the job of a cowboy? On ranches in the American West, traditionally cattle (cows and bulls) lived freely on a wide area of land. Cowboys would round them up and bring them back to the ranch when necessary, mark them, and do various other work necessary on the ranch. The job required riding horses for long distances and skill in catching and controlling cattle. To test and compare their skills in these areas, a competition called the rodeo became popular.

When ranches started to have financial problems, they found that offering tourist services was more profitable than farming. The word "dude" is now a cool name to call people, and is popular in the surfing community. But originally it referred to people from the city who had no experience riding horses. Thus, a dude ranch is a place where people can come and experience the life of a cowboy for a few days.

A main activity on a dude ranch vacation is horseback riding, and guides take you on scenic trails. Some dude ranches hold cattle drives for the real cowboy experience, and guests can try their hands at guiding cattle. Watching a rodeo is another traditional activity. But a lot of the charm is in staying at the ranch in the atmosphere of the Old West, and eating traditional foods.

To attract more customers, dude ranches have been adding a wider variety of tourist activities, from hunting and fishing to tennis and golf – to even massages and yoga. It's incredible to imagine, though, that what now may be a resort experience with a rustic atmosphere has been a tourist tradition for over 130 years, since before even Western movies were made.

## Words

| | | | |
|---|---|---|---|
| bull 雄牛 | rodeo ロデオ | horseback 馬に乗った | scenic 景色の良い |
| trail 人・動物が通ってできた小道 | | charm 魅力 | rustic 田舎の |

## Comprehension

1. Write numbers to show the order in which these first appeared.

   _____ the job of cowboys  _____ Western movies  _____ dude ranches

2. Find one dude ranch on the internet and fill in the information.

   Location: _____

   Activities: _____

3. A rodeo is a competition for _____.

   a. cowboys to show off skills they develop as a hobby

   b. dudes to try ranch skills

   c. cowboys to compare skills they use in their jobs

   d. cowboys who wish to appear in Western movies

4. Originally, was the word "dude" positive or negative? _____

5. Write T for True, or F for False.

   _____ Dude ranches were originally based on the images in Western movies.

   _____ One job of cowboys is to steal cattle from other ranches.

   _____ Actually, cowboys don't ride horses much.

   _____ Dude ranches have changed throughout the years.

## Vocabulary Focus

| guide | core meaning: 導く | （動）案内する |
| --- | --- | --- |
| | | （動）導く、進ませる |
| guided missile: its direction can be changed while flying. So, people can guide it to the target. guide dog: a dog that guides its master | | （動）指導する |
| | | （動）（思想，感情が）動かす、支配する |
| | | （名）案内人、ガイド |
| | | （名）旅行案内書、入門書 |
| | | （名）目印、目安 |

guideを適切な形にして以下の文を完成させましょう。

1. I _____ the visitors to the nearest exit.

2. When you don't know what to do next, take a look at the _____.

3. Teachers don't just teach facts, they also _____ students in their plans for the future.

4. I've always wanted to be a tour _____ in a famous city.

5. There are signs and other _____ to help you find the campus.

**1.** Dude Ranchで休暇を過ごすと楽しそうだと思うことと、自分に合わないと思うことをパッセージから探して、表に書きましょう。

| Good points | Bad points |
|---|---|
| 例）learn to ride a horse | |

**2.** これらの良い点と悪い点を考えた上で、以下の質問に答えましょう。

Would you like to take a vacation at a dude ranch?　□　Yes.　□　No.

**3.** YesまたはNoを選んだ理由を2つ書いてみましょう。自分の好みや気持ちについての理由が良いでしょう。そして、それぞれの理由の下に、関係する点を1から写して書きましょう。

| Reason: (Noの場合の例) no interest in horses | Reason: | Reason: |
|---|---|---|
| Support: <br><br> • main activity is horseback riding <br><br> • traditional activity is watching a rodeo | Support: | Support: |

**4.** グループになってアイディアを共有しましょう。

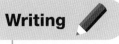

Topic: Would you like to take a vacation at a dude ranch?

**5.** このトピックについて自分の考えを選んでください:

☐ I would like to take a vacation at a dude ranch.

☐ I would not like to take a vacation at a dude ranch.

**6.** 3のReason/Supportのボックスをもとに、理由と二つのサポートを完全文にします。必要な場合は説明を加えましょう。

| |
|---|
| Reason:<br>no interest in horses. |
| Support:<br><br>• main activity is<br>  horseback riding<br><br>• traditional activity is<br>  watching a rodeo |

Reasonを完全文にする:

I am not interested in horses.

Supportの一つを<u>完全文にして</u>、<u>必要な場合説明を加える</u>:

**The main activity at a dude ranch is horseback riding,** and I don't want to participate in it.

もう一つのサポートも同じように書く:

Also, **a popular event is watching a rodeo.** At this event, cowboys show their skills riding horses.

3で書いたボックスから同じように文を書いてみましょう。

Reason: _____

Support 1: _____

Support 2: _____

Reason: _____

Support 1: _____

Support 2: _____

**7.** パラグラフの形にしてみましょう。パラグラフの順は:

● 5で選んだ文がtopic sentenceになります。

● 6で書いた文の順で続きます。それぞれの理由の前に**First, Second,**を付けます。また、それぞれの二つ目のサポートには**Also,**をつけます。

● concluding sentenceとして、topic sentenceに"**For these reasons,**"を付けて繰り返します。

# *Writing Focus* 英語のパラグラフの構成

英語のライティングの構成は、日本語の構成とは異なります。日本語で書く時は日本語の構成、英語を書く時は英語の構成を使いましょう。

英語の構成はサンドイッチのように、一つのテーマの具が2枚の同じパンに挟まれています。

日本の構成はお弁当のように、いろいろなアイディアが含まれていて、一つ一つを味わう面白さがあります。

There are three reasons why small cars are better than big cars. First, they are more fuel efficient, so they are better for the environment. Second, they are convenient because you can park them anywhere. Third, they are much less expensive to buy and maintain. Considering the environment, convenience, and economy, small cars are the best choice.

Topic sentence（大体は最初の文）とConcluding sentence（最後に来るまとめになる文）は同じことを伝える。これが、具を挟むパンの役割になる。

トピックをサポートする文は「具」になる。ツナサンドを作りながら途中でハムサンドの具も加えたりしないように、決まった一つだけのテーマにする。

パラグラフというのは段落のことですが、英語の段落は日本語よりも長いことを忘れないようにしましょう。特に、一文だけのパラグラフを書かないように気を付けましょう。

**Let's Try!** Writing（p.65）で書いたパラグラフを見て、構成を考えてみましょう。Topic SentenceとConcluding Sentenceはほとんど同じことを伝えられているか、そして、サポートの文にはそのトピックに関係がないものが入っていないか確認しましょう。

# Unit 11  Shirley Temple

**Conversation Box:**

❖ Which child actors are popular now? In the recent past?

❖ What happened to some child actors when they became adults?

## Do you know these words?

すでに知っている単語の□にチェック印✓を書いて、下に単語の意味を書きましょう。次に分からない単語の意味を辞書で調べて書きましょう。

☐ inspire      ☐ memorize      ☐ permission      ☐ delegate      ☐ ambassador

_____ _____ _____ _____ _____

★パッセージを読むとき、ここで書いた意味がパッセージで使われている意味と合っているかどうかを確認しましょう。

# Shirley Temple

**44** These days, we may only see the name Shirley Temple on the menu at a restaurant or bar, but our grandparents may remember the girl who inspired this non-alcoholic cocktail. Shirley was an excellent dancer and child star, appearing in movie after movie and inspiring people in the difficult time of the Great Depression. 5

**45** Shirley was born in 1928 in Los Angeles. Her mother sent her to dancing lessons from the age of three. Living in the Hollywood area, she was scouted to act in ten-minute short films featuring all young children. Due to her dancing ability and personality, but also possibly due to her ability to follow instructions on stage at a young age, she soon went on to feature films and starring roles. 10

**46** Working as an actress at such a young age was not easy. She couldn't read yet, so instead of fairy tales, every night her mother read the movie script to her. They practiced her lines until she fell asleep. The director's punishments were harsh when child actors did not cooperate, and she couldn't rest even if she had an injury or fever. When she was old enough for school, a private teacher gave her lessons 15 during free times on the movie set.

**47** But Shirley loved dancing and acting. She always wanted to arrive early on the set to watch and talk with the stage hands preparing for the shoot. She became friends with all of them. She memorized not only her own lines, but the lines of all of the actors. 20

**48** As she approached superstar status, life changed in many ways. Her family hired a bodyguard for fear of her being kidnapped. Many items were being sold showing her picture without permission. And vicious rumors circled – that she was not a child but an adult dwarf, that she was wearing a wig, and that she was not trained in dance. The latter was hardest on her, as her skill in dancing was the result of years 25 of hard work.

**49** Temple acted in a few movies as an adult, but she soon left Hollywood and entered politics and government. She served as America's delegate to the United Nations, the ambassador to Ghana, and the ambassador to Czechoslovakia. She contributed all throughout her 85-year life in a wide variety of ways, but will 30 probably most be remembered for the dimpled pout and curly blonde hair of her years as a child star.

## Words

| | | | | |
|---|---|---|---|---|
| fairy tale 童話 | script 台本 | punishment 罰 | harsh 厳しい | kidnap 誘拐する |
| vicious 悪意のある | rumor うわさ | dwarf 小人 | dimple えくぼ | pout ふくれっ面 |

## Comprehension

1. Write numbers to show the order in which these happened in Shirley Temple's life.

_____ Shirley's family hired a bodyguard.

_____ A private teacher started to give Shirley lessons on the movie set.

_____ She became the ambassador to Ghana.

_____ She learned how to read.

_____ She started dancing lessons.

_____ Shirley was given her first starring role.

_____ Vicious rumors circled about Shirley.

_____ Shirley practiced her lines with her mother at night.

2. On the internet, find one video clip of Shirley Temple dancing. Write your impression of it: _____

3. Write T for True, or F for False.

_____ "Shirley Temple" is the name of a cocktail, but it has no alcohol in it.

_____ When she was very young, dancing was the only skill that she had.

_____ While appearing in movies, Shirley was able to have a normal child's lifestyle.

_____ Shirley Temple was kidnapped only once while she was famous.

## Vocabulary Focus

| **line** | core meaning:　線 | （名）線、しわ、境界、前線 |
|---|---|---|
| | | （名）列 |
| along the lines of　の基本線に沿って | | （名）ひも、電話線 |
| draw the line at　境界を引く | | （名）行、せりふ |
| out of line　規則に従わないで | | （名）路線 |
| read between the lines　行間を読む | | （動）線を引く、並べる |
| toe the line　言われたとおりにする | | （動）裏打ちする |

それぞれの文のlineの意味を選択肢から選びましょう。

1. _____ Call anytime, our lines are always open.
2. _____ Everyone, take out a piece of lined paper.
3. _____ My coat is warm because it's lined with wool.
4. _____ There's always a long line in front of that shop.
5. _____ What's the meaning of "them" on line six of the passage?

| A. 列 |
| B. 線を引く |
| C. 電話線 |
| D. 行 |
| E. 裏打ちする |

## Thinking about the Topic

**1.** パッセージから、Shirley Templeが子役で良かったこと、大変だったことを整理しましょう。

| Good points | Bad points |
|---|---|
| 例）became a Hollywood star | |

**2.** 他の子役について調べて、成功や苦労をまとめてみましょう。

| Child Actor | Good/Bad Points | Career as Adult |
|---|---|---|
| | | |
| | | |
| | | |

**3.** 子役になると良いことと、悪いことを他にも考えてみましょう。

64

## Writing

Topic: Should parents encourage their children to become stars?

◆Topic sentence

4. 1～3で集めた情報を見て、自分の考えに合うトピックセンテンスを選んでください：

☐  Parents should encourage their children to become stars.

☐  Parents should not encourage their children to become stars.

◆Supporting sentences

5. 1～3で使いたい具体例を、分野別にReason①と②に分けて整理しましょう。例のように、複数の子役の具体例を使うと、説得力のあるサポートになります。また、①と②のサポートセンテンスのバランスを調整して、トピックセンテンスが全体的に説得力のあるパラグラフになるよう、計画しながら書きましょう。

| Reason: (Noの場合の例) It's important to grow up with other children. | Reason①: | Reason②: |
|---|---|---|
| Support: <br><br> • Temple didn't attend school with other children. <br><br> • In junior high, Candace Cameron attended school for two hours every day to find some friends. | Support: | Support: |

6. 今度はワープロソフトを使ってパラグラフを書いてみましょう。書き方は次ページのコラムにあります。パラグラフの流れは：

➢  4で選んだ文 (Topic sentence)

   ↓

➢  5で整理したことを完全文にして、

   First, Reason① + Support sentence × 2

   Second, Reason② + Support sentence × 2　の順で書く。

   ↓

➢  まとめの文 (Concluding sentence)を4のTopic sentenceをもとにして書く。

*Writing Focus*

# ライティングの提出方法：ワープロソフトを使用する場合

ワープロでのライティングの元は手書きのフォーマットなので、基本が同じです。

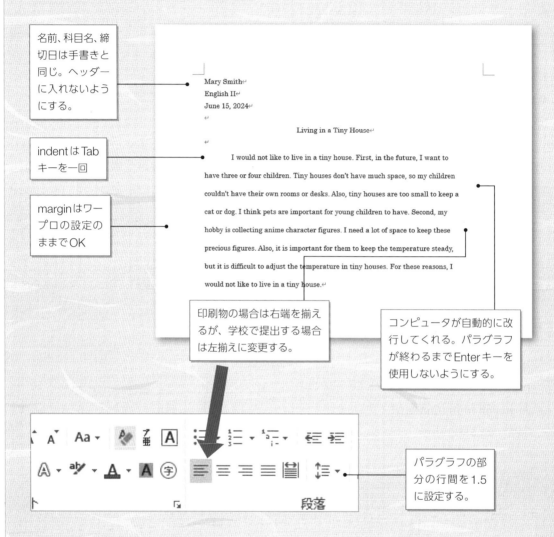

名前、科目名、締切日は手書きと同じ。ヘッダーに入れないようにする。

indent は Tab キーを一回

margin はワープロの設定のままで OK

Mary Smith
English II
June 15, 2024

Living in a Tiny House

I would not like to live in a tiny house. First, in the future, I want to have three or four children. Tiny houses don't have much space, so my children couldn't have their own rooms or desks. Also, tiny houses are too small to keep a cat or dog. I think pets are important for young children to have. Second, my hobby is collecting anime character figures. I need a lot of space to keep these precious figures. Also, it is important for them to keep the temperature steady, but it is difficult to adjust the temperature in tiny houses. For these reasons, I would not like to live in a tiny house.

印刷物の場合は右端を揃えるが、学校で提出する場合は左揃えに変更する。

コンピュータが自動的に改行してくれる。パラグラフが終わるまで Enter キーを使用しないようにする。

パラグラフの部分の行間を1.5に設定する。

段落

■提出チェックリスト：
☐ 印刷する時は新しい1枚の紙に印刷する。提出までに折ったり汚したりしないようにする。
☐ 2枚になった場合は、両面印刷をせずに2枚で提出する。
☐ オンライン提出の場合はワープロソフトのドキュメントを添付する。

**Let's Try!** このフォーマットを使い、前ページのパラグラフをワープロソフトを使用して書いてみましょう。

# Unit 12 — The Pink Tax

## Conversation Box:

❖ Do you compare prices before you buy something?

❖ Do you like items made specifically for your gender, or neutral items?

## Do you know these words?

すでに知っている単語の□にチェック印✓を書いて、下の意味と線で結びましょう。なお、分からない単語があれば辞書を使って、全ての単語を線で結びましょう。

□ tendency   □ compound   □ purchase   □ cosmetics   □ consideration

● 化粧品   ● 買う   ● 傾向   ● 考慮   ● 悪化させる

# The Pink Tax

The pink tax is a problem in the U.S., Britain, and several other countries, but it is not a tax per se. A tax is a surcharge on goods that is paid to the government. The pink tax, however, refers to the phenomenon that women must spend more money than men in their daily lives.

Hearing this, you may think that it is a natural result of the differences in their lifestyles. For example, it is reasonable that a fashionable haircut for a woman is more expensive than a simple haircut for a man. Also, women's clothing requires more cloth and intricate sewing than men's clothing. And, women spend money on make-up and beauty products, while many men simply wash their faces before going out. A difference in cost would therefore seem unavoidable.

However, this difference is just one minor aspect of the pink tax. Research into the pink tax focuses on items that are exactly the same, yet the version for women is sold in pink packaging and costs more. For example, one study found that a pack of razors cost $4.99, and a pink package of the exact same razors was $6.99. Such marketing was found in personal hygiene items, clothing, and even tools. Children's items were also affected, with pink toys, pink clothing, and pink baby goods being priced higher than those for boys.

The above tendency of women to require more expensive items compounds the problem. There are many costs that women face. They must purchase menstrual items, cosmetics, and more. While a good haircut and make-up may seem to be a personal choice, it has also been found that a woman may not succeed in her career if she does not take care with her appearance.

Taking into consideration the wage gap, in which women are paid 17.7 percent less than men, women bear a heavier burden than men do in the modern world. In particular, this affects single mothers and the poor. It poses a unique problem because there is not just one cause or organization to blame. We need to come up with creative solutions to deal with this inequality in society.

## Words

per se 本質的に　　surcharge 追加料金　　phenomenon 現象　　razor かみそり
personal hygiene items 衛生用品　　menstrual 月経　　burden 負担

## Comprehension

1. Which of these is not part of the "pink tax"?
   a. The same item being sold "for women" being more expensive.
   b. Money paid to the government.
   c. Women buying more beauty products than men do.
   d. Fashionable women's haircuts costing more than simple men's haircuts.

2. Complete this sentence about the passage.
   Women bear a heavier burden than men due to these three factors: higher _____ for products sold to women, the need to _____ more expensive items, and the gender _____ gap.

3. Why can't women simply choose a less expensive lifestyle?
   a. It is embarrassing to buy products sold for men.
   b. They don't have enough information about this situation.
   c. Not investing in personal appearance may affect their career.
   d. Spending money is an important part of their identity.

4. Several products were given as examples of women's items costing more than neutrally packaged versions. Find one more item that is compared in articles or web pages on the pink tax.
   Item: _____     Price: _____
   Women's Price: _____

## Vocabulary Focus

| **pose** | core meaning:<br>ポーズ | （動）引き起こす |
|---|---|---|
| | | （動）問いかける |
| ※一時停止のポーズ（pause）と発音、意味が違う<br>　ので注意すること | | （動）ポーズをさせる、ポーズをとる |
| | | （動）ふりをする |
| pose a question: 問題を投げかける | | （名）ポーズ |
| pose for a painting: 絵画のためにポーズをとる | | （名）気取り、格好つけ |

poseを適切な形にして以下の文を完成させましょう。

1. Global warming _____ a threat to us all.
2. His interest in children's welfare is just a _____.
3. He _____ for the painter for over three hours.
4. First, I would like to _____ a question to all of you.
5. She _____ as a security guard to enter the building.

1. ネットや店舗で日本で販売されている商品の値段を調べましょう。男性用、女性用、男女兼用のものを比べましょう。

| Item, Shop | Men's Item Price | Women's Item Price | Neutral Item Price |
|---|---|---|---|
|  |  |  |  |
|  |  |  |  |
|  |  |  |  |
|  |  |  |  |
|  |  |  |  |
|  |  |  |  |
|  |  |  |  |

2. 男性専用、女性専用の商品とその値段を比べましょう。

| Items Necessary for Men | | Items Necessary for Women | |
|---|---|---|---|
| Item | Price | Item | Price |
|  |  |  |  |
|  |  |  |  |
|  |  |  |  |
|  |  |  |  |
|  |  |  |  |
|  |  |  |  |

## Writing 🖊

Topic: Is there a pink tax in Japan?

### ◆Topic sentence

3. 1〜2で集めた情報を見て、自分の考えに合うトピックセンテンスを選んでください：

A: Japan, too, has a pink tax.

B: Japan does not have a pink tax problem.

C: Japan does not have a pink tax. Rather, it has a blue tax.

### ◆Supporting sentences

4. 以下の表から3で選んだA,B,Cに対する二つの理由文を使ってください。
それぞれをサポートする具体例を前ページから選んで、完全文で書きましょう。

| Your Stance | A | B | C |
|---|---|---|---|
| First Reason | Some women's items are more expensive than others. | Women's items are not more expensive than other items in Japan. | Some men's items are more expensive than others. |
| Second Reason | Women have to spend more money on items for their daily life. | Men and women spend about the same amount of money on daily life items. | Men have to spend more money on items for their daily life. |

●具体例の書き方 例（1）：

どこで　　　　　　　　　　　　商品　　　　　　値段　　　　　商品　　　　　　値段

| At Papa Mart in Chuo-ku |, | men's towels | are | 650 yen |, but | neutral towels | are | 450 yen |.

| On the Big Chance website |, | both men's and women's work gloves | are | 680 yen |.

●具体例の書き方 例（2）：

Necklaces are more expensive than neckties.

Only women have to buy cosmetics.

5. パラグラフの形で書いてみましょう。パラグラフの流れは：

- 3で選んだ文 (Topic sentence)
  ⬇
- "First, ..." ＋理由1＋具体例 (Supporting sentences)
  ⬇
- "Second, ..." ＋理由2＋具体例 (Supporting sentences)
  ⬇
- まとめの文(Concluding sentence)

◎3で選んだトピックセンテンスの前にpink taxを説明する一文を足すと、より分かりやすいパラグラフになります。

Writing Focus

## 英語の手紙もサンドイッチ

ライティングだけではなく、英語の手紙や電子メールもサンドイッチの構成になる。

最初の文では手紙のトピックと目的を伝える。
英語では、日本語の手紙やメールによくある書き出しを使うと、誤解が起きる場合もある。

| このように始まると | **My name is...** | **季節の挨拶** | **Thank you for your work.** |
|---|---|---|---|
| このような内容の手紙だと思われる | 自己紹介中心の手紙。ペンパルのリクエストにも使うが、よく見かけるのはDMや募金活動なので続きを読まない人もいる | 特に用事がないことを伝える。後回しにするかもしれないので、大事な話の場合は困る | 今までのことに関して感謝を伝えることがテーマなら…もしかしてクビ？と心配する部下もいる |

良い手紙・メールの書き出しは、相手と自分の関係に触れながら手紙の目的を伝えること：

| 感謝を伝えるようなことがある場合 | 感謝を伝えてから要件を書く | Thank you for the lovely meal last week. Concerning the contract we spoke about,... |
|---|---|---|
| 久しぶりの場合 | そのことに触れてから要件を書く | It has really been a long time since we last saw each other. How have you been? Today... |
| 特別なことがない場合 | 相手の健康を願ってから要件を書く | I hope you are doing well. Today I am writing to you because... |

上記のように相手のことで始まる場合は、手紙・メールの最後にも、書き出しと関連するような挨拶で終わると良い。これがサンドイッチの反対側のパンの要素になる。

Thank you for the lovely meal. → I hope I can treat you to a meal sometime soon.
It has been a long time → I hope we can get together sometime soon.
I hope you are doing well. → Best wishes on all of your endeavors.

**Let's Try!** 英語の先生に課題についての質問がある場合、メールの書き出しの文として一番適切なものを選びましょう。
a. My name is Keiko Tanaka.
b. I'm a student in your English I class, and I have a question about the homework.
c. We are starting to see the leaves change color as the days get cooler and cooler.

# Unit 13    Product Placement

## Conversation Box:

❖ Have you noticed popular products in movies and TV shows?

❖ Do you want to buy a product after you see it in a movie?

## Do you know these words?

すでに知っている単語の□にチェック印✓を書いて、下の意味と線で結びましょう。なお、
分からない単語があれば辞書を使って、全ての単語を線で結びましょう。

☐ placement      ☐ sum      ☐ brief      ☐ budget      ☐ aware

● short    ● amount    ● money to spend    ● know about    ● putting somewhere

# Product Placement

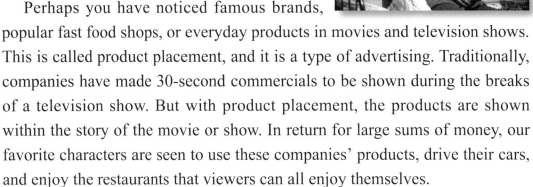

Perhaps you have noticed famous brands, popular fast food shops, or everyday products in movies and television shows. This is called product placement, and it is a type of advertising. Traditionally, companies have made 30-second commercials to be shown during the breaks of a television show. But with product placement, the products are shown within the story of the movie or show. In return for large sums of money, our favorite characters are seen to use these companies' products, drive their cars, and enjoy the restaurants that viewers can all enjoy themselves.

Product placement has become a big business in recent years. There are specialists whose job it is to match a company's products with new movies and TV shows. Viewers don't want to see actors trying to sell products when they are enjoying a movie, so writers fit the products into the story to make it seem natural. There are various degrees of placement available. Some companies just have their logo shown in the background, but for more money the product can be talked about in the dialog or used by the characters. Even more money puts the product in a pivotal scene, or introduces its features.

Of course, the appearances of products in movies and TV shows are very brief. Many viewers do not even notice them. Nonetheless, many companies have had success when using this type of advertising. Viewers start to associate the brand with the characters and actors, and in the cases of some very popular movies, sales of the products have risen dramatically.

It is easy to associate product placement with modern trends in advertising. However, it has actually existed for a long time. Famous authors from the 19th century such as Charles Dickens, Jules Verne, and Jane Austen included products in their novels in return for payment. In a famous Manet painting, we can clearly see bottles of Bass beer. Both then and now, artists need funding. Better productions can be made with bigger budgets. But as viewers it is important for us to be aware that these items are being shown to us as advertisements.

## Words

pivotal 回転の軸となる、極めて重要な

74

## Comprehension

1. Product placement _____
   a. shows the product on screen for less time than TV commercials.
   b. has only one method of showing the product.
   c. costs much less than other kinds of advertising.
   d. is always successful in increasing product sales.

2. From articles or web postings, find an example of product placement in Japanese media.

   Movie or TV show: _____

   Product or brand: _____

3. Why do writers try to fit the product into the story well?
   a. It's easier to see the product that way.
   b. Viewers don't like to feel that something is being advertised.
   c. They receive more money for doing it well.

4. Write T for True, or F for False.

   _____ Product placement has been used for a long time.

   _____ Writers try to emphasize the product in the movie or TV show.

   _____ People always notice the products that are put in movies and TV shows.

   _____ Some product placements have been very successful.

## Vocabulary Focus

| **brand** | core meaning:<br>銘柄、ブランド | （名）銘柄、ブランド、商標、商品 |
| --- | --- | --- |
| | | （名）種類 |
| name brand: ブランド商品 | | （名）焼き印 |
| brand-name: ブランド名の | | （動）焼き印を押す |
| brand-new: 新品の、真新しい | | （動）[不幸な経験などが]心に焼きつく |
| brand loyalty: 同じ銘柄の商品を買い続ける | | （動）汚名を着せる |

brandを適切な形にして以下の文を完成させましょう。

1. After the incident, the boy was _____ as a coward.
2. Our shop carries various _____, catering to everyone's preferences.
3. _____ cattle is one of the jobs of a cowboy.
4. The image of the fire was _____ into her memory.
5. It isn't my favorite _____, but I'll take it.

1. Product Placementの良い点と悪い点を整理しましょう。

| Product Placement Merits | Product Placement Demerits |
| --- | --- |
| | |

2. ある会社の商品を、どのように宣伝するか会議で決めることになりました。グループに
分かれて、半分はCMで、半分はProduct Placementの立場になり、メリット、デメリッ
トを挙げながらディスカッションをしてみましょう。

## Writing 🖊

**Topic: What are the merits and demerits of product placement for advertisers?**

3. 次ページのコラムで紹介する複数のパラグラフのエッセイを書きましょう。最初と最後のパラグラフができているので、2番目のパラグラフにメリットを、3番目のパラグラフにデメリットを書いてください。複数のメリットとデメリットを書くようにしましょう。

### Product Placement

Sometimes we see everyday products in movies or television series. This is called product placement, and it is a way that companies advertise their products. There are both merits and demerits to this method of advertising.

There are several merits to using product placement for a product. First, _____

_____

_____

_____

_____

_____

_____

_____

_____

There are also several demerits to product placement. First, _____

_____

_____

_____

_____

_____

_____

In this way, there are both merits and demerits to product placement as a method of advertising. A company needs to consider its budget, message, and target audience in order to decide which method is best for its product.

## Writing Focus

## 複数パラグラフのライティング構成

複数のパラグラフを書く際も、1段落のみのパラグラフを書く時と基本的な構成は変わりません。

長くするために、書くことをただ増やしていくのではなく、それぞれのパーツがサンドイッチのような形になるよう、パラグラフを進化させる必要があります。

一文ずつになっているTopic sentence, Concluding sentenceを、複数の文のパラグラフにするには、トピックの紹介などを付け足します。Supporting sentencesには説明や具体例を増やし、それぞれをパラグラフにします。

---

There are three reasons why small cars are better than big cars. **First,** they are more fuel efficient, so they are better for the environment. **Second,** they are convenient because you can park them anywhere. **Third,** they are much less expensive to buy and maintain. Considering the environment, convenience, and economy, small cars are the best choice.

---

Purchasing a car is a very personal endeavor, and everyone has their own preferences. There are luxury cars, sports cars, offroad vehicles, and family cars. But most cars can be divided into two categories of size – large and small. Of the two, small cars have several advantages over large cars.

**First,** small cars are more energy efficient, so they are better for the environment. It takes more gasoline or electricity to move a large, heavy car. So, to go the same distance, more energy is used. This adds up over time, making a difference in our ecological footprint.

**Second,** they are convenient because you can park them anywhere. Many people drive larger cars, so parking places for small classed cars are often available when others aren't. It's also much easier to maneuver them into tight spots. You might even be able to have a smaller driveway at your home, saving space for other things you want to do on your land.

**Third,** they are much less expensive to buy and maintain. In addition to gasoline and electricity, other costs are also lower. Taxes are a big cost when owning a car, and these are lower. There also tend to be fewer luxury accessories.

Considering the environment, convenience, and economy, small cars are the best choice. The popularity of large cars is evident by the number that we see on the road wherever we go. Let's not add to the problems these cars are causing while gaining personal benefits that only a small car can offer.

---

**Let's Try!** ユニット8, 9, 10で書いたパラグラフの中でどれか一つ選び、文章を長くする方法を考えてみましょう。

# Unit 14  Toki Pona

**Conversation Box:**

❖ What is most difficult about learning a foreign language?

❖ Do you prefer high context or low context communication?

## Do you know these words?

すでに知っている単語の□にチェック印✓を書いて、下に単語の意味を書きましょう。次に分からない単語の意味を辞書で調べて書きましょう。

□ theory      □ structure      □ concentrate      □ combine      □ context

_____    _____    _____    _____    _____

★パッセージを読むとき、ここで書いた意味がパッセージで使われている意味と合っているかどうかを確認しましょう。

# Toki Pona

*pilin ike*  *telo lete*  *kala lili*  *toki pona*

59　There is a theory that a person's worldview is shaped by the structure of the language that he or she speaks. In light of this idea, linguist and translator Sonja Lang created the language Toki Pona in 2001. She hoped that by concentrating on basic things, the language could promote positive thinking.

60　The sounds, words, and grammar of Toki Pona are based on English, Chinese, Esperanto, and several European languages. It therefore should feel familiar to people in many parts of the world. Care was also taken to use sounds that are easy to pronounce for people of many backgrounds. But the main feature of the language is that it is minimalist. There are only 137 words and 14 letters. The words cover basic concepts, and other words are made by combining these. For example, bathroom is *tomo* ("room") and *telo* ("water").

61　Another feature of the language is that it is high context. This means that a lot of details are not said, and the meaning is known only through the situation around the speakers. For example, there are no tenses. Whether someone is saying, "I ate the apple," "I am eating the apple," or "I will eat the apple," cannot be known through only the words spoken. To understand, we look to see if the speaker is eating now, or whether or not the apple still remains uneaten. In addition, items are usually referred to through their categories. Fruits are usually just called *kili* ("fruit or vegetable"), and a combination is used only when the difference needs to be shown, such as *kili telo* ("fruit" + "water") for watermelon.

62　The lack of specificity makes translation of contracts or scientific papers impossible, but has an interesting effect on daily conversation. We need to pay close attention to the situation and the speaker's thinking. It sharpens our minds, and helps us understand others more.

63　Toki Pona was registered as a language with the International Organization for Standardization (ISO) in 2022. Since 2001, there has been a growing online community of Toki Pona learners and speakers. Over 160 people claim to speak it fluently, and there are books, web magazines, music, and more in the language. As popularity of this language grows, it is hoped that a positive outlook will also spread around the world.

5

10

15

20

25

30

## Words

linguist 言語学者　　minimalist ミニマリズムの　　tense 時制　　specificity 明確さ
ISO 国際標準化機構

## Comprehension

1. The lack of verb tenses is an example of _____ .

   a. positive thinking

   b. minimalism

   c. high context

2. The passage introduces the Toki Pona words *tomo*, *telo*, and *kili*. Search the internet to find one more Toki Pona word and its meaning in English.

   Toki Pona word: _____ Meaning: _____

   From these four examples, do Toki Pona words seem easy to pronounce?

   _____

3. Write T for True, or F for False.

   _____ Toki Pona is not appropriate for contracts and scientific papers because its words' meanings are too broad.

   _____ There are no native speakers of Toki Pona.

   _____ We can only talk about basic concepts when we use Toki Pona.

   _____ Sonja Lang was the first person to discover this language.

## Vocabulary Focus

| **claim** | core meaning:<br>**主張する** | （動）主張する、自分にあると主張する |
|---|---|---|
| | | （動）[人命]を奪う |
| ＊日本語の「クレーム」のニュアンスは英語のclaimと違います。「クレーマー」は英語だとclaimantで、意味は「要求する人、主張者」です。 | | （動）[保険金の]支払いを請求する |
| | | （名）主張 |
| | | （名）要求 |
| | | （名）権利、資格 |

それぞれの文のclaimの意味を選択肢から選びましょう。

| | | |
|---|---|---|
| 1. _____ The flood claimed the lives of hundreds of people. | A. 主張する |
| 2. _____ The man claims that he is innocent. | B. 奪う |
| 3. _____ He has no claim to the land that he is living on. | C. 主張 |
| 4. _____ You won't receive the insurance unless you make a claim. | D. 要求 |
| 5. _____ We didn't believe her claim because she gave no evidence. | E. 権利、資格 |

1. トキポナを国際共通語として導入する良い点と悪い点を考えてみましょう。実際に世界の国で教育現場や国際関係の場で使用する際の、トキポナの特徴のプラスとマイナスの面を整理しましょう。

| （例）simple words, sounds, grammar | Good:<br>● （例）only 120 words, can learn quickly |
| --- | --- |
| | Bad:<br>● （例）children don't experience the difficulty of learning other languages |
| | Good: |
| | Bad: |
| | Good: |
| | Bad: |
| | Good: |
| | Bad: |

2. このテーマで、クラスまたはグループでミニ・ディベートをしてみましょう。

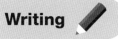

**Writing**

Topic: Should Toki Pona be adopted as the official world-wide lingua franca?

**3.** 以下のエッセイにSupporting sentenceのパラグラフを1つまたは2つ書いて、エッセイを完成させましょう。最後のパラグラフには、書いたパラグラフのポイントを付け足して完成させましょう。

### Toki Pona as Lingua Franca

Toki Pona is a minimalist language created in 2001. Registered as an official language in 2022, it is based on languages around the world. There are several reasons why this language should be taught in all countries and adopted as the official world-wide lingua franca.

First, using Toki Pona as a lingua franca is fair to everyone. This language was created, so there are no native speakers. It is a foreign language to everyone in the world. Therefore, everyone will have the same opportunities to become fluent. One country will not have a dominant role because the lingua franca came from its culture.

Second, _____

_____

_____

_____

_____

_____

_____

_____

_____

_____

_____

_____

In these ways, Toki Pona is perfect as the official world-wide lingua franca. It is fair to everyone, _____

_____

_____

**14**

Toki Pona

## Writing Focus

### 主題文：Topic Sentence

パラグラフの始まりにはtopic sentenceというトピックを提示する文があります。

● **トピックをフルで書くことが大事**

> **My Mother**
>
> She is important to me for three reasons. First,...

> **My Mother**
>
> My mother is important to me for three reasons. First,...

タイトルでトピックが伝わっていても、主題文には全ての情報を含めるようにします。

> Topic: Do you agree or disagree that the minimum wage should be raised?
>
> Yes, I do. I have three reasons. First,...

> Topic: Do you agree or disagree that the minimum wage should be raised?
>
> I agree that the minimum wage should be raised. I have three reasons. First,...

課題のテーマが決まっていても、主題文ではそのテーマについて繰り返し書きます。

● **トピックとは直接関係がない背景の情報で始まらない**

> I am a university student in Japan. I have five brothers and sisters. Living in a big family has many advantages. First,...

> Living in a big family has many advantages. First,...

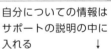

自分についての情報はサポートの説明の中に入れる　↓

上の例だと "living in a big family" よりも、自分と、自分のファミリー中心のテーマとして読み手に伝わってしまいます。

● **主題文と関係がない文がパラグラフ中にないように気を付ける**
それぞれの文が、直接主題文をサポートしているか確認しましょう。

**Let's Try!**

主題文として一番適切な文を選びましょう。
a. Tokyo is a great place to live for three reasons.
b. I agree with this opinion for three reasons.
c. Human rights is an issue that has been important to me for a long time.

# The CSI Effect

### Conversation Box:

❖ Do you enjoy watching TV shows about crimes and police work?
❖ Do fictional TV shows that you watch seem realistic?

## Do you know these words?

すでに知っている単語の□にチェック印✓を書いて、下の意味と線で結びましょう。なお、分からない単語があれば辞書を使って、全ての単語を線で結びましょう。

☐ commit      ☐ evidence      ☐ determine      ☐ conflict      ☐ contribute

● 決定する      ● 犯す      ● 対立する      ● 証拠      ● 貢献する

# The CSI Effect

One popular genre of television series is the police procedural. Many enjoy watching detectives try to find out who committed a crime. This may seem like harmless entertainment, but this kind of program has been found to be changing our society. It is called the CSI effect, named after *CSI: Crime Scene Investigation*. This series was very popular from 2000 through 2015. In it, not detectives but forensic scientists, or crime scene investigators, collect evidence, test it, and interview witnesses to solve cases.

The main way that the CSI effect has been changing society is in the courts. Juries have a higher faith in physical evidence such as fingerprints or hair. In *CSI* and many crime series, guilt is determined by a perfect match of DNA. However, in real life, such evidence is not always available, and a 100 percent match is impossible. Further, many of the scientific techniques used in these series do not exist. Jurors therefore tend to believe defendants if there is no physical evidence, and decide against them when physical evidence conflicts with witness testimony.

A second effect is in how criminals commit crimes. By showing police solving crimes, real criminals get ideas for how to avoid this. In several cases, criminals have been more careful about leaving fingerprints and DNA such as hairs. And by showing various cleverly planned crimes in each episode, criminals get ideas for their own crimes. In this way, some unsolved crime statistics have increased.

A third effect is that many young people have become interested in careers in crime scene investigation. Traditionally, university forensic science courses were only available at the graduate level, but now short undergraduate courses are available. As a result, many applying for forensic science jobs have less experience and general scientific knowledge than before. Also, there is a higher rate of people quitting such jobs. The television shows make the job look exciting, but actually a forensic scientist merely repeats laboratory work without knowing the details of each case. Unrealistic expectations may have led many to choose a career that does not fit their interests and skills.

While the CSI effect is named after *CSI*, a large number of past and present television series are contributing to these phenomena. When watching television, it is important to remember that it's not just the stories that are fictional. Details about police procedures and science may also differ from reality.

## Words

procedural 手続き型　forensic 科学犯罪捜査の　jury 陪審　guilt 有罪　juror 陪審員
defendant 被告　testimony 証言　graduate 大学院　undergraduate 大学の学部課程

86

## Comprehension

1. Complete the sentence about how the CSI Effect has changed our society.

   Because of the CSI Effect, jurors have higher requirements for physical _____, _____ are better at committing crimes, and _____ has become more popular at universities.

2. Research the name of another police procedural that features forensic science.

   Television series name: _____

3. Write T for True, or F for False.

   _____ In police procedurals, evidence is collected and trusted more than in real life.

   _____ Jurors believe evidence more than they believe witnesses.

   _____ New crime scene investigators have more educational training than before.

   _____ The job of crime scene investigator is less interesting than what is shown on TV.

## Vocabulary Focus

| **court** core meaning: 中庭 | (名) 法廷、裁判所 |
|---|---|
| | (名) 裁判官 |

| "囲まれた場所"というのが原義です。<br>そこから、以下のように派生してcourtが使用されるようになりました。<br>―宮廷：大きな敷地で囲まれた場所<br>　├中庭：宮廷の庭<br>　├コート：かつて中庭に存在したことから<br>　└法廷・裁判所：かつて裁判は宮廷で行われたことから<br>派生語には以下がある。<br>　├courteous 礼儀正しい　courtly 上品な<br>　└courtship 結婚前の交際期間 | (名)（スポーツのための）コート |
|---|---|
| | (名) 宮廷 |
| | (名) 中庭 |
| | (動)（結婚を前提に）交際する |
| | (動) 機嫌をとる |

それぞれの文のcourtの意味を選択肢から選びましょう。

1. ____ The court denied the defendant's request.
2. ____ A player loses a point if they hit the ball out of the court.
3. ____ She showed little interest in any who courted her.
4. ____ Members of the royal court have various duties.
5. ____ The Supreme Court only hears cases that come from lower courts.

| A. 裁判所 |
|---|
| B. 裁判官 |
| C. コート |
| D. 宮廷 |
| E. 交際する |

## Thinking about the Topic

1. CSI Effectはどのように社会に影響を及ぼしてきたか、以下にまとめてみましょう。

| TV Series Content | Effects |
|---|---|
| (例)<br>crime series show perfect matches of DNA evidence | (例)<br>● juries believe DNA evidence too much<br>● |
|  |  |
|  |  |

2. 他のジャンルのテレビドラマでブレーンストーミングをしてみましょう。それぞれのドラマに間違った内容がある場合に、社会へ及ぼす影響を想像してみましょう。

| Genre | Possible Effects on Society if Unrealistic |
|---|---|
| (例) Hospital Series |  |
|  |  |
|  |  |

## Writing ✏️

Topic: Should broadcasters be prohibited from showing unrealistic or untrue content in fictional television series?

**3.** 以下のエッセイは、このトピックに関して「禁止すべきではないが、より気を付けるべき」という立場の意見になっています。誤解を引き起こすようなドラマと、その影響についてのパラグラフを書いて、エッセイを完成させましょう。CSI Effectとその例、そしてもう一つ、他のジャンルのドラマの例を必ず入れましょう。

### Realism in Television

Unrealistic depictions in television productions are having negative effects on society, and it has been proposed that laws should be made to rectify the situation. I understand that this is a serious problem, but I disagree with the idea of making laws against it.

Lack of realism in television series can affect many aspects of our society. First,

_____

_____

_____

_____

_____

_____

_____

_____

_____

_____

_____

However, there are many reasons why laws should not be used to solve this problem. First, a law restricting content to realistic depictions would violate freedom of expression. This has been recognized as a human right by the United Nations. Second, it would make a lot of fictional content less entertaining. Waiting several months for DNA results in a crime series, or not being able to include time travel in a science fiction show would limit television shows too much. The purpose of entertainment is to take viewers away from the real world.

Some unrealistic television content is having bad effects on society, but it would be a mistake to deal with this by making laws. Producers need to face this issue and find solutions in voluntarily limiting dangerous misrepresentations, or by adding disclaimers. Viewers can encourage such actions by voicing their concerns. In this way, I believe the issue should be faced without resorting to making changes in the law.

*Writing Focus*

## 結論文：Concluding Sentence

パラグラフの終わりにはconcluding sentenceという結論を伝える文があります。

● **トピックをフルで書くことが大事**

> These are the reasons for my opinion.

> These are the reasons why I believe that the minimum wage should be raised.

○

トピックをもう一度フルで書きましょう。Topic sentenceとほとんど同じでも構いません。

> In conclusion, they need support from various people in order to succeed.

×

> In conclusion, student athletes need support from various people in order to succeed.

○

分かりやすいので代名詞でも大丈夫だと感じる箇所も、必ず元の名詞を使って書きましょう。

● **伝えたばかりの理由を中心的に書かないように気を付ける**

> In conclusion, living in a big family is great because we are never alone.

> In conclusion, living in a big family is great because there are many to share household duties with, we can learn social skills, and we are never alone.

○

● **パラグラフのコンテンツ以上のことを書かないこと。**

自分のことが話題になっていない時に、結論文だけに自分のことを入れないようにする：

　　× I am thankful to all of the members of my family every day.

将来のことが話題になっていない時に、結論文だけに今後のことを入れないようにする：

　　× I hope to have a big family someday.

また、結論文の後にもこのような文を加えないようにしましょう。

**主題文：Tokyo is a great place to live for three reasons.**

この主題文で始まったパラグラフに対して、結論文として一番適切な文を選びましょう。

a. These are the reasons why I hope to live in Tokyo someday.

b. This is a great place because of the variety of people, transportation convenience, and availability of international goods.

c. In conclusion, Tokyo is a great place to live because of the people, transportation, and shopping.

# Idea Garden
## First Steps in Paragraph Writing

検印
省略

©2023 年 1 月 31 日　初版発行

編著者　　　　　　　　　　　Magda L. Kitano

発行者　　　　　　　　　　　小川洋一郎

発行所　　　　　　　　株式会社　朝日出版社
〒101-0065 東京都千代田区西神田3-3-5
電話　東京　(03) 3239-0271
FAX　東京　(03) 3239-0479
e-mail　text-e@asahipress.com
振替口座　00140-2-46008
www.asahipress.com
組版／メディアアート　製版／錦明印刷

ISBN978-4-255-15706-1